Also by Mark Weiss

Published By Books For Better Living

THE HANDBOOK FOR FREE MATERIALS
ON ORGANIC FOODS

ENCYCLOPEDIA OF VALUABLE FREE
THINGS FOR BRIDES AND
YOUNG MARRIEDS

1,000 FREE THINGS TO HELP YOU KEEP
YOUR MATE IN LOVE WITH YOU

1,000 FREE MATERIALS ON LOVE,
SEX AND MARRIAGE

501 FREE COOKBOOKS, RECIPES
AND MENU IDEAS

501 VALUABLE TIPS and FREE MATERIALS FOR MOTORISTS

by Mark Weiss

BOOKS FOR BETTER LIVING • CHATSWORTH, CALIFORNIA

Copyright © 1974

BOOKS FOR BETTER LIVING
21322 Lassen Street
Chatsworth, California 91311

All Rights Reserved.

No portion of this book may be reproduced in any form without permission in writing from the publisher, except by a reviewer who may quote brief passages as a part of his review.

PRINTED IN THE UNITED STATES OF AMERICA

ISBN 0-87056-342-4

Library of Congress Catalog Card Number:
73-90015

ACKNOWLEDGMENT

I am most grateful to the editorial staff of "The Best Things In Life Are Free!" for their assistance in the preparation of this book. I am especially grateful to my assistant, Louisa Berson.

We are also very grateful to Ralph Nader's Center For Auto Safety for giving us permission to offer to readers all of their excellent reports, letters, press releases and other information of value to automobile owners.

Last, but definitely not least, our thanks to Davis Publications, publishers of *Autofacts*, for granting us permission to pass on to you some of the outstanding money-saving tips in their book.

CONTENTS

INTRODUCTION 9
HOW TO USE THIS BOOK 13

SECTION ONE:
HOW TO SAVE MONEY

Chapter 1
   New Cars 17

Chapter 2
   Pros and Cons of Leasing 30

Chapter 3
   Buying A Used Car 33

Chapter 4
   Know Your Car 42

Chapter 5
   Saving Money On Maintenance 45

Chapter 6
   Tire Economy and Safety 53

Chapter 7
   Safety Equipment 62

Chapter 8
   Buying Auto Supplies 69

Chapter 9
> Automobile Insurance 72

Chapter 10
> Save On Financing 79

Chapter 11
> The Internal Revenue Service
> Can Help You 84

SECTION TWO: CONSUMER PROTECTION

Chapter 12
> Government Specifications For
> Your Vehicle 89

Chapter 13
> Advice From The Federal Trade
> Commission 96

Chapter 14
> How To Protect Yourself Against
> Auto Fire and Theft 103

Chapter 15
> Ralph Nader and The Center For
> Auto Safety Reports 106

Chapter 16
> Consumer's Directory 129

APPENDIX
> Free Films For Drivers 157

INTRODUCTION

The United States Federal Highway Administration has just released a report to consumers showing that it will cost the average owner of a 1973 standard size automobile $13,552—without considering inflation—to operate and maintain the vehicle over the anticipated ten years of the life of the car.

That breaks down to almost 14 cents a mile. But that is just the beginning. Costs have already started to rise over the 14 cents per mile figure as new requirements are passed into law, and as the costs of parking, repairs, insurance, tires, tolls and so on keep going up all the time.

So how long will it be before each one of our cars is costing us 20 or 25 cents a mile to operate?

According to one transportation expert whose report appeared in newspapers coast-to-coast recently, it has already happened for many families!

Even if you are only a one-car family, one or two big repair bills can make a considerable dent in the family budget—not to mention skyrocketing insurance bills or even an accident.

Now the question is: What can we do about it? What can you and I, as individual automobile owners, do about cutting down on the costs of automobile ownership? Well, it took several thousand questionnaires and letters, but we found out there are definitely things you can do, not only to reduce the cost of owning an automobile but to insure you and your family safe driving.

We were amazed at the results of the mailings we made to experts all over America. The response was very gratifying and very helpful, otherwise we would never have been able to write this consumer protection guide for automobile owners and buyers.

Most amazing of all to us was the fact that so much material is available absolutely free of charge! Free? Today? Is there really anything that is free today? The answer is yes—if you know *where* and *how* to get it and if all the arrangements are made for you in advance.

That is just one of the purposes of this book: to bring helpful free materials to your attention and, at the same time, to arrange in advance for you to be able to send for everything you want at no cost to you except for some postage.

Actually, this book has been written so that it is really three books in one, and can serve you in three different ways:

1. As a source of supply guide.
2. As a guide to free things.
3. And as a consumer protection guide for automobile owners.

Because there has never been a book like this

published before, we had to start from scratch by writing to thousands of business associations, nonprofit groups, state and federal government agencies, manufacturers, educational institutions and so on. In addition, we read and clipped many hundreds of items from newspapers and magazines.

It is from the flood of responses from all of these sources that we were able to compile this much-needed book.

Most important, we found that these sponsors are *anxious* for you to send for, read and use their free materials. The reason for this is that these sources want to acquaint you with their products and services and the best way for them to do that is to offer you something valuable enough so that you will want to write to them for it, use it and keep it after you receive it. This is how they get to know you and vice versa.

The materials you receive from these sponsors are truly free because you are *not* obligated in any way to buy anything.

Now you have at your fingertips many reliable sources of extremely helpful free materials for automobile owners.

We wish you the very best of success in the years to come in controlling skyrocketing automobile ownership costs—and we hope this guide will help you to better enjoy being an automobile owner, for less money and with more protection and safety.

HOW TO USE THIS BOOK

1. All the free materials listed in this book are bona fide offers. They represent the "cream" of the free things that are available from business, industry, non-profit organizations, associations and government agencies.

2. The sponsors of the free things assured us in writing that they will be happy to supply these items in good faith. However, each sponsor reserves the right to discontinue or withdraw its offer whenever it sees fit. They will honor all requests until their supply becomes exhausted. They also reserve the right to substitute other materials in place of those listed herein.

3. When making a request, it is very important to print your full name and address clearly, and include your zip code. If your zip code is missing, your request may not be filled.

4. Allow approximately four to six weeks for processing and delivery. Some material will reach you sooner and some may take longer. (Requests for U.S. Government publications sometimes take several months to fill because of huge demand.)

5. If you use postcards, please make certain that your printed name, address and zip code appear on the blank side of the postcard, not on the stamped side.

6. Please respect special conditions. If a long self-addressed and stamped envelope is required, send one, with an eight-cent stamp attached. If there is a small charge to cover part of the postage and handling costs, do not ignore this stipulation. Remember, you are getting something valuable. Recent large increases in postage, printing and handling costs have forced some sponsors to request a small postage and handling charge.

7. Please do not write the publisher or to us for any of the free materials. Address all requests directly to the sources listed. It is not possible for us to process and reply to large numbers of letters requesting information and material. We cannot insure that you will receive everything you send for. We cannot assume the responsibility that everything you request will be sent to you because the sponsors have reserved the right to discontinue or withdraw their offers at any time.

8. There are additional bonus offers free to you! Many sponsors have more than one free thing available—some have dozens and some have hundreds! Thus, this book will lead you to many

more free things that are not listed herein. This is our added bonus to you!

SECTION ONE

HOW TO SAVE MONEY

Chapter 1

New Cars

VALUABLE INFORMATION FOR POTENTIAL NEW CAR BUYERS!

The gigantic aura of interest surrounding the introduction of new automobiles is rekindled each year when the first new shiny models come rolling off the Detroit assembly lines amid considerable pomp and publicity. As soon as these cars hit the street, thousands of otherwise sensible Americans go flocking to the showrooms from coast to coast to get a close-up look at the glittering new motorized creations. Then they cast disgusted looks at the three year old models sitting in the driveways and begin dreaming of buying one of the spanking new cars.

Even though you are partially assisted by the mammoth advertising campaigns tossed at you by the major automobile manufacturers, just knowing what the cars look like and kicking a few tires is scarcely enough for a smart buyer. A new car may appeal to you esthetically and mechanically, but if you want to get the most for your money, you have to be concerned with price.

As everyone knows, buying a new car is a major investment and knowing what is a good price to pay for a car is not always easy, especially when you must deal in a market that is full of mystery, confusion and sometimes even deception. Examples: A dealer can tell you his sticker price is your final price or if you're lucky, take a few dollars off. Yet he'll sell the same car to another buyer for hundreds of dollars less because that buyer knows something that you don't; that is, he knows what the car cost the dealer. And suppose the dealer tells you he's giving you a bargain. Just for you he's going to slash the price to $250 over cost. How do you know? How can you be sure he isn't still taking a neat $1,000 profit? Even if he cuts the price of the car, how do you know he isn't inflating the option prices?

You had no way of knowing until *Car/Puter*.

Car/Puter is a consumer price protection service operating in conjunction with United Auto Brokers, Inc. Car/Puter's unique service combines sophisticated computer technology, vast purchasing power and a select national dealer network making it possible for you to purchase most new automobiles for only $125 above dealer's cost. Your automobile is delivered to you from participating dealers in your area complete with pre-delivery service and warranty.

Now! Buy any brand new car for only $125 over dealer's cost through Car/Puter!

Now you can buy your new car knowing as much about the confidential dealer prices as the Detroit auto makers because Car/Puter reveals exactly what the dealer himself pays the factory for the car you want and the optional equipment you select

HOW CAR/PUTER WORKS!

For $7.50, Car/Puter will send you their New Car Yearbook. It is part of their comprehensive service. It is crammed full of pictures and helpful information about the new models, the latest changes, and the optional equipment available. Now you can compare!

When you have decided on the make and model you want—now or 6 months from now—simply complete and mail the appropriate Car/Puter Model and Equipment Form which is provided in the back of your New Car Yearbook. It lists all the options available and equipment packages being offered on the model of your choice.

There are many other buying services that offer you new cars at $100 to $125 above dealer cost—but often you have to settle for another model and do not receive the specified optional extras. Car/Puter offers you the model you specify and the optional extras indicated.

Car/Puter's basic service is a computer printout of itemized dealer cost and retail price for the car you specify with optional extras. This valuable information gives you bargaining power.

If you don't want to spend time going from dealer to dealer trying to bargain, you can buy the car of your choice, with optional extras, directly from Car/Puter at $125 above dealer cost.

PROS AND CONS
1. Car/Puter gives you a bona fide price.
2. You get a true price list for the model you choose and all options. This gives you bargaining power.
3. You wait, on the average, one to two months for delivery. It is possible to get a car immediately if you are flexible.
4. The distance you have to travel to pick up your new car may be over 50 miles.
5. You have to sell your old car yourself. Sometimes, and quite often, you get a better price if you do sell your old car yourself.
6. You may have a problem getting satisfactory warranty service in your area.
7. With many low-priced cars, under $3,000, the dealer markup may not be enough to justify Car/Puter.

If you want more information, write, without

obligation, to Car/Puter for the following free pamphlets:
1. Buying A New Car? Save Up To $1,000 Or More!
2. Free reprint of an article about Car/Puter from *Changing Times!*
3. Questions and Answers About Car/Puter and United Auto Brokers!
4. Step-By-Step Instructions On How To Use Car/Puter Services!
5. A letter explaining what Car/Puter's service is!
6. A diagram of all of the information covered in a Car/Puter price quotation!

THE OWNER'S MANUAL CAN PROVIDE YOU WITH VALUABLE INFORMATION!

Even before you purchase a new car, *read the owner's manual.* The facts and figures within the manual can provide you with valuable information and help you decide whether or not it is the car for you.

VALUABLE PERFORMANCE DATA FOR NEW CARS AND MOTORCYCLES!

The National Highway Traffic Safety Administration has published three booklets providing comparative performance information about cars and motorcycles:
1. Brakes: A Comparison Of Braking Performance For Passenger Cars & Motorcycles

2. Performance Data: New Passenger Cars and Motorcycles
3. Tires: A Comparison Of Tire Reserve Load For Passenger Cars

The booklets are compiled from data provided by domestic and foreign manufacturers of cars and motorcycles. "Tires" and "Brakes" rank cars according to their stopping ability. "Performance Data" does not rank cars, but it does provide figures for each make and model indicating performance in acceleration and passing ability. The booklet also includes tire and braking information and tire maufacturers' codes for marking tires.

Information about each make and model car and motorcycle is also available from new car dealers. They must provide customers and potential customers with performance data about the cars or motorcycles they display and offer for sale. Thus, to get information to compare cars, consumers must go from dealer to dealer.

If you want to study the booklets before you shop, all three booklets are available from:
Superintendent of Documents
Government Printing Office
Washington, DC 20402

"Brakes" costs 55 cents; "Tires," 65 cents; "Performance Data," $2.85.

FOREIGN VS. AMERICAN CARS

Foreign-built automobiles apparently held a lead over American cars in braking effectiveness and tire strength, the National Highway Traffic Safety Administration reported. The agency made public three booklets in its fourth annual study of comparative performance information on new cars and motorcycles.

Two of the booklets rank all current models from best to worst in stopping ability and tire reserve load, and the other includes a third performance category, acceleration and passing ability.

The consumer publications are furnished each year to identify certain safety features in new model cars and motorcycles, and as an aid to prospective buyers, Douglas W. Toms, Safety Administrator said.

The comparative rankings are based solely on information which the manufacturers supply to us. Foreign-make cars occupy the top seven positions in braking performance, and the top sixteen positions in tire reserve load.

BUYING A CAR ABROAD REQUIRES FORETHOUGHT!

American visitors to a foreign country who plan to buy a car there and ship it home would be wise to first read a new government booklet. "Importing A Foreign Car" explains shipping, duties, licensing, and clearance procedures in simple terms.

Keep in mind that a resident may apply his $100 duty-free exemption toward the value of the car only under conditions. Also, a car entering this country must comply with U.S. emission standards, and it's up to the buyer to make sure his new car does.

Get your booklet by including 10 cents for postage and handling and writing to:
Consumer Product Information
Washington, D.C. 20407

REGULATION TO AID CAR BUYERS!

Beginning January 1, 1972, a regulation went into effect to aid persons shopping for a new car.

The Transportation Department amended Federal Motor Vehicle Safety Regulations on Consumer Information, making it easier to obtain safety information about new cars.

Consumers are now able to obtain and take home information that previously was available only in dealer showrooms.

In the past, safety information was available in showrooms to explain a new car's stopping distance, acceleration and passing ability, and tire reserve loads. It had also been available to purchasers of new cars.

The Transportation Department says the purpose of the regulation is to enable shoppers to get information free of charge and to keep it for use in comparing cars on a safety basis. If you don't want to go to a showroom, you may get information on each make and model by mail by requesting it from dealers or manufacturers.

FREE GUIDE MAKES YOU AWARE OF PHONY ADS!

Good advertising often means good selling. It does not necessarily mean true advertising. Protect yourself against dealers who advertise one thing and try to sell you another. Ask for your free copy of "Guard Against Phony Ads."
Federal Trade Commission
6th St. & Pennsylvania Ave., NW
Washington, D.C. 20580

FREE ILLUSTRATED LIST OF COMMON DECEPTIONS!

Here's what to look for so you won't be one of the many victims of deceit. This free booklet is a list of invaluable illustrations the consumers should be aware of to avoid being deceived. Ask for your free copy of "List of Common Deceptions." Write to:
Federal Trade Commission
6th St. & Pennsylvania Ave., NW
Washington, D.C. 20580

FREE CONSUMER GUIDE GUARDS YOU AGAINST FRAUD!

"Don't be Gypped," Booklet No. 8, outlines and details deceptive practices, misleading marketing, fraudulent advertising and common consumer problems. For this excellent narrative description

of each phase of consumer protection, write to:
Federal Trade Commission
6th St. & Pennsylvania Ave., NW
Washington, D.C. 20580

FREE CONSUMER EDUCATION GUIDE: DECEPTIVE ADVERTISING OF GUARANTEES!

Now you can find out what guidelines industries follow to avoid deceptive advertising of guarantees. If you are a well-informed consumer you will not be among the many who are gypped every year. Ask for "Guides Against Deceptive Advertising of Guarantees."
Federal Trade Commission
6th St. & Pennsylvania Ave., NW
Washington, D.C. 20580

FREE CONSUMER EDUCATION GUIDE: GUARD AGAINST DECEPTIVE PRICING!

You may not be saving as much as you think you are! A sale is not always a sale and that holds true for automobile purchases. Now you can find out the guidelines the FTC sets for industry. Ask for "Guides Against Deceptive Pricing."
Federal Trade Commission
6th St. & Pennsylvania Ave., NW
Washington, D.C. 20580

FREE STAFF REPORT FROM THE FTC!

You can obtain a free staff report on the documentation auto manufacturers submit to the FTC. This documentation substantiates any advertising claims made by the automobile industry. Write to:
Federal Trade Commission
6th St. & Pennsylvania Ave., NW
Washington, D.C. 20580

NEW CAR: BUY OR LEASE?

The automobile is often a necessity and is the consumer's second most important purchase—a house ranks first. In 1971 alone, according to the Commerce Department Survey of Current Business, 46.7 billion dollars was spent on cars and their parts and another 23.7 billion on gasoline and oil. Cars and car parts accounted for 7 percent of all consumer spending, with gasoline accounting for an additional 4 percent.

What these figures mean in terms of your pocketbook is the subject of a Transportation Department study, "Cost of Operating an Automobile". According to this study, the total cost of owning and operating a standard size car for 10 years is approximately $13,553; a compact car, $10,808; and a subcompact car, $9,444. Depreciation is the largest single factor in these costs—32 percent for a standard size car, 24 percent for a compact car and 21 percent for a subcompact car. Other costs included in these figures: repairs, maintenance, replacement tires, accessories, gas and oil, insurance, parking, tools, taxes and fees.

To avoid some of these costs, many consumers have turned to an alternative to car buying—car leasing. Long term leases are now being offered by major car rental companies and many independent companies. Two types of leases are usually available: full service leases and net finance leases (names and details of leases may vary somewhat from company to company). Under the full service lease, the monthly rental charge includes repairs, maintenance, insurance, and replacement tires. Under the net finance lease, you pay all the same costs you would if you owned the car, except for the initial outlay, registration, and titling.

The following are factors that should be considered when deciding between leasing or buying:

1. The size of the car. Lease rates, purchase prices and operating costs vary greatly with different car sizes. Be sure to compare lease and purchase prices of the same size car.
2. The length of time you intend to keep the car. Depreciation costs can amount to as much as 50 percent of the purchase price of the car in the first two years of ownership. By leasing you may be able to avoid some car depreciation losses.
3. Whether the lease terms permit you to buy the car at the end of the lease period. By purchasing the car at this time you can avoid

the large initial capital outlay needed to buy the car new and can buy a used car, with yourself the only previous driver.
4. The amount of driving you intend to do and the costs of insurance in your area. The chief advantages of the full service lease are that all your repairs, maintenance and insurance costs are included in the higher monthly rental charge. But true savings from including these services in a lease may occur only if you drive your car more than a certain mileage per year or live in an area where insurance rates are high.
5. Personal property taxes levied on cars by some cities and states.

A summary of the Transportation Department study, "Cost of Operating an Automobile," is available free from:

Consumer Product Information
Washington, D.C. 20407

Chapter 2

Pros and Cons of Leasing

LEASING VS. BUYING?
WHICH IS CHEAPER?
If you are looking for a new car but can't lay out the initial down payment, leasing may be the answer for you.

Many of the major car-leasing firms now offer long-term leases.

TWO TYPES OF CAR LEASING
The first type of lease is the full service lease which includes the monthly rental charge covering repairs, maintenance, insurance and replacement tires. The other is the net finance lease where you pay all the costs as if you owned the car except you do not pay for the initial outlay, registration and titling.

THINGS TO CONSIDER WHEN LEASING!
Rates, prices and operating costs differ greatly with car size. Compare prices of cars of the same size.

When you lease you can avoid some depreciation losses. Should you decide to purchase the leased car, someone else pays for depreciation. And you buy a "one owner" car.

Full service leases offer you the advantage of repairs, maintenance and insurance costs. However, you do pay a higher monthly lease charge.

You decide the make and model without actually purchasing the car. The rental firm owns it; you are only leasing it.

Less of your own capital is tied up in a leased car. That money can be put to work for you in other areas.

To obtain a lease car you have to have an excellent credit rating. Your driving record must be good, you must show that you could afford to buy a new car and that you drive a minimum of 10,000 miles a year.

Leasing an automobile is just as expensive as owning it in terms of monthly payments.

You must sign a contract for at least 6 months to one year. You may not want or need the rental car for that long a period. You cannot cancel your lease and return the car.

When your lease is up, you have nothing of value to show for the money you've spent. If you had purchased the car you would at least have something of value.

The difference between renting and leasing is renting is short-term and leasing is long-term. Many of the same rules apply to both. Consider how much you will be using the car to determine whether leasing or buying is better for you.

Make sure a luxurious big car is really worth the extra cost. You may be better off leasing a small economy car.

Go shopping before you lease a car. Compare leasing costs, deals and terms. Find the best for your individual needs.

You may be charged for mileage if you drive a car more than was specified in the leasing contract.

Make sure the insurance coverage provided by your leasing contract is adequate.

It is usually more profitable for a company to lease a car than it is for an individual to lease.

Remember, only *you* can determine whether leasing or buying is best for you. Check all the angles before you lease or buy. It could save you a lot of money.

UNCLE SAM COMPARES LEASING AND PURCHASING!

"Cost of Operating an Automobile" is an excellent booklet from the Transportation Department. It compares leasing costs with the cost of owning a car. You can obtain a copy of this valuable booklet, free, by writing to:
Consumer Product Information
Washington, D.C. 20407

Chapter 3

Buying A Used Car

HERE'S HOW YOU CAN GET THE BEST BUY ON A USED CAR!

If you buy after a snow storm you have a very good chance of getting a good deal. Few people will venture out during or right after a snow storm so you are the only prospect a commission-seeking salesman has. December and January are the best months for buying a used car.

NEVER BUY WHEN IT'S RAINING OR AT NIGHT!

A steady drizzle can make even the worst paint job look good. And don't buy at night, no matter how well-lit the used car lot is. Trust only the sun for revealing paint and body flaws.

CHECKLIST OF ITEMS TO LOOK FOR ON THE LOT!

1. View the body of the car at an angle, looking for rippled surfaces; they are an indication of a paint job to hide repair work.

2. Paint on the chrome and rubber sealing strips indicate a paint job to cover signs of a major accident.
3. Scratch around the lower edge of the body to check for rust; also check door sills and the inside of the trunk.
4. Check everything that is supposed to move. Operate the doors, windows, high and low headlights.
5. Look for a sagging door or misaligned trunk; these are signs of damage from a crash.
6. Sagging seats or broken springs, worn-through or brand new rubber on pedals and floor mats and discoloration on steering wheel are proof of excessive wear, mileage and abuse.
7. Press the brake pedal for at least 30 seconds; if there is an easing down you will be repairing brakes sooner than you ever hoped.
8. Make sure the steering wheel doesn't move more than two inches in either direction while the car is standing still.
9. Start the engine and listen carefully for peculiar noises when you run through the gears.

CHECKLIST OF ITEMS TO LOOK FOR ON THE ROAD!

1. Pull the car up a few feet; check the ground underneath for oil or water leaks.
2. Take the car out on the road and make the engine work by fast acceleration (about 15 mph to around 55 mph). Decelerate to 15

mph and give the accelerator a strong push. If you see blue or dark smoke from the tailpipe, it is an indication the piston rings are worn and a large repair bill is in store for you.

THE BEST CHECK ON A USED CAR IS A MECHANIC!

The best way to check your prospective purchase is to let a qualified mechanic check it out. Arrange an appointment with him in advance (never on a weekend). For approximately $10 he will spend an hour looking over the car on a hoist. He will check the wheels, universal joints and other parts. Try to arrange a deal with a mechanic. He checks the car out and you bring it to him for repair and service.

FIND OUT WHO THE PREVIOUS OWNER WAS!

Always ask the dealer for the name, address and telephone number of the previous owner. If he refuses to reveal who the previous owner was—beware—of both the car and the dealer. You can save yourself money and trouble if you go to a more reputable dealer.

BUYING A USED CAR FROM A RENTAL FIRM!

Rental firms are a good source for late-model used cars. As new models come out, rental firms begin selling last year's models. The average mileage on these cars is approximately 15,000. Rental cars are usually sold to individual purchasers. To find out if rental cars are available in your area, call the managers of fleet sales and purchases for local rental firms. Rentals are *usually* good buys.

However, there are some rental cars which have been driven 50,000 to 75,000 miles. These cars are also put into the used car market. They are hard to spot and often have had their outsides touched up and the odometers turned back; all you're getting is a goodlooking "junkmobile". If you follow the tips given in this book on used cars, you should be able to avoid getting stuck with a lemon.

SET A PRICE BEFORE YOU BUY A USED CAR!

Don't venture onto a used car lot unless you have a set price you can pay. After you set this price, look around and see what is available for that price. Remember—interest rates for used cars are higher than those for new car purchases.

IT PAYS TO BUY A CAR IN DEMAND!

When you buy a car in demand you are sure of getting a better price when you decide to sell it. The following are cars now in demand:

Economy Cars: Pintos, Toyotas, Vegas, Gremlins and Volkswagens.

Intermediate-Sized Cars: Chevelle, Torino, Comet, Montego, Matador, LeMans, F-85, Skylark, Satellite and Coronet.

The hottest moving item on the lots today are light-weight trucks. They are also the hardest to obtain.

THERE IS SAFETY IN SIZE!

Because economy cars are so in demand, many used car dealers are making very good offers on the bigger standard models. They are the best buy from a safety standpoint. A recent spokesman for the American Association for Automotive Medicine said, "Get the biggest 1967 or later car you can find." Important safety equipment became standard on 1967 and later models. There is a greater chance of injury or death when a small car becomes involved in an auto accident.

A CLUNKER IS NO BARGAIN!

Clunkers do not pass the inspection required in most states without putting out more than the car is worth. Don't buy foreign makes if the manufacturers have a limited American dealer organization or an insufficient distribution of parts. Some foreign car engines are not made to withstand long, continuous high-speed driving. And high-performance cars are not bargains if they have been abused by their previous owners.

HOW CAN YOU BE SURE YOU'RE GETTING A FAIR PRICE?

The best way to check is a *Blue Book* list of wholesale and retail prices for used cars. You can find blue books at the library. Ask your local banker or insurance agent if you could browse through his copy. You can try asking the used car dealer to let you look at his copy, but chances are you won't get that opportunity. Most prices, whether from a dealer or a private seller, are inflated. This makes for bargaining between seller and buyer.

BEWARE OF LATE-LATE MODELS!

Few pepole trade or sell their cars before they are two or three years old. Often, a car for sale that is only one or two years old has either been in a wreck or classifies as a lemon. This does not mean that you can't get a good used car one or two years old, but it is best to be very careful.

STATION WAGON OWNERS ARE PRACTICAL!

Be cautious when considering the purchase of a late model station wagon. Wagon owners usually keep their cars much longer than other car owners and these cars are very popular with salesmen and other long-distance travelers. If you are looking for a used station wagon, don't use the odometer as your guide.

BUYING A USED CAR PERSON-TO-PERSON!

You can save money if you buy person-to-person because you eliminate the middleman. But there are some risks you take in buying privately. Car dealers are licensed and controlled by local and state government agencies. You risk the possibility of a lien on the car when you purchase from a private seller.

The advantage of having a warranty is forfeited. You pay the price and hope the car is all the private seller said it was.

You do not have the advantage of assistance in obtaining financing. Buying privately usually means cash on the line.

Buying from friends or relatives gives you the opportunity of purchasing a car you know has been properly serviced and maintained.

HOW TO CHOOSE A REPUTABLE USED CAR DEALER!

Find out how long the dealer has been in business before you buy from his lot. An established dealer with a good reputation is a better choice than a slick fast-talking fly-by-night dealer who hits low-income areas and runs.

"No down payment" is a sure sign of a dealer interested in quantity rather than quality. Most reputable dealers do little or no advertising—they depend upon their reputation.

WHAT ABOUT CAR AUCTIONS!

Avoid them! They're just for experts who can spot a good deal quickly. You don't get time for a thorough inspection and you can't take the car for a test drive. Unless you know what you're looking for and what to look for (which means you would have to be a pretty good mechanic), stay away from car auctions.

WHEN BUYING A USED CAR . . .

A new federal regulation requires the seller of a used car to give the buyer a written statement of true mileage. But if the car has had two or three previous owners, how can you tell whether the odometer has been turned back? Experts say telltale signs of mileage greater than that shown on the odometer include excessive wear on the pads on the brake pedal and accelerator, frayed arm rests and badly worn carpeting. As a precaution against getting a car in bad condition, you could take it to a diagnostic clinic if one is available. Or you could have your mechanic check the car.

MILEAGE LISTING IS A MUST!

If you buy a used car from a dealer or from a private seller, be sure to get a certified statement that the mileage shown on the odometer is accurate to the best of his knowledge.

Under a federal regulation you, the buyer, can

sue with intent to defraud, if the odometer reading is proven to be incorrect.

Chapter 4

Know Your Car

GET TO KNOW YOUR NEW CAR!
The more attention you give your new car the more it will serve your needs. Open the hood and study the engine while it is still new. Turn the engine on and listen carefully to the sounds it makes when it is in good condition. Treat your car like a good friend.

STUDY YOUR POWERHOUSE WHILE IT IS STILL NEW! FOLLOW THIS CHECKLIST OF PARTS YOU SHOULD GET TO KNOW!
1. Fan and generator belts; note tension.
2. Local reservoir for windshield cleaner.
3. Check the amount of liquid in the battery cells.
4. Locate the oil dip stick and learn how to read it.
5. Find the fuse panel; be sure you have a spare fuse for each.
6. Examine the jack; test its operation.

HOW TO REFILL YOUR WINDSHIELD CLEANER RESERVOIR!

The cost of refilling your windshield cleaner reservoir at a service station is usually one dollar. You can do the same by mixing a concentrated detergent made for this purpose with water. By locating the windshield cleaner reservoir, you can refill it yourself for pennies.

ALWAYS KEEP SPARE FUSES OF EACH VALVE USED!

You may find yourself on a back road in the middle of the night and your lights are out. You can replace the fuse in seconds if you have studied the fuse panel and have a spare fuse on hand.

TEST THE JACK BEFORE YOUR FIRST BLOWOUT!

The jack in your new car may not work the same as the jack for your old car. Your first flat is not the time to experiment with a new jack. You can save yourself time and inconvenience just by knowing how your new jack works.

TUNE IN TO YOUR CAR'S BEHAVIOR!

Study your car while it is still new. Listen to its sounds, learn how it takes bumps, get the feel of the brakes. While your car is new, condition yourself to counteract small, but significant changes in performance. Don't wait until a major breakdown occurs! Investigate and correct immediately.

WHAT TO DO IF YOUR CAR TAKES BUMPS POORLY!

If your car reacts poorly to bumps, most likely you need shock replacements. In the case of air shocks, you may need them pressurized. If you are not concerned about a rougher ride, you should be concerned if your car has extra sway. It could jeopardize your steering capability.

Chapter 5

Saving Money On Maintenance

HERE'S HOW YOU CAN CUT DEPRECIATION!

Ultimately, you will spend three times the amount you paid for your car to run it. And you won't save money on transportation by trading for a new car every year. The key to cut depreciation is day-to-day maintenance.

ECONOMY AND LUXURY CAR OWNERS TAKE CARE!

Whether you have invested in an economy car for its low mileage or a luxury car for prestige, gasoline and repairs climb ever upward. One way to cut down on repairs and often get more mileage is to undertake an everyday check under the hood.

If you have ever stalled on the expressways or late at night, you will appreciate a car that runs well. Only daily maintenance can provide you with the convenience of mobility that you are entitled to from your car. Don't blame your car for troubles you could have avoided. Take good care of your car!

FIND OUT HOW WAXING CAN CUT DEPRECIATION!

About every three months it is a good idea to wax your car. It not only keeps it looking good, but it protects the paint from flying grit and sand. It also provides protection against the acid-eating action of dead insects.

WHAT IS A WARRANTY DEED? IF YOU DON'T KNOW IT MAY COST YOU MONEY!

Read the Warranty Deed from beginning to end. Especially the section on *owner's responsibilities*. This section details responsibilities that you as the owner must live up to. You can lose all claims stated in the warranty deed if you fail to carry out your responsibilities. Another very good reason why daily maintenance is so important to you and to your car.

CHECKLIST OF MANDATORY MAINTENANCE PROCEDURES!

1. Dates and odometer mileage readings
2. Engine oil change
3. Chassis lubrication
4. Check fluid levels
5. Change engine oil filter
6. Change automatic transmission fluid
7. Replace positive crankcase ventilator valve

8. Replace air cleaner element
9. Drain and flush the cooling system

These maintenance procedures may vary for different types of cars, but in general these are typical mandatory maintenance procedures. A form is often provided with these maintenance requirements stated. If so, post it where you can see it daily. Or use this list as your guide.

DAILY MAINTENANCE CAN PROVE BENEFICIAL WHEN YOU DECIDE TO TRADE-IN!

The difference of several hundred dollars is part of the price you might pay if you have neglected daily maintenance. When you decide to trade-in the car you presently own for a new one, remember you could have gotten a better trade-in price if your old car had been in better condition. Start your daily maintenance program today.

PATRONIZE A PROFESSIONAL SERVICEMAN!

No matter how qualified your moonlighting repairman might be, he is not an established, professional serviceman. The importance of a qualified serviceman can save you money. Whether you choose to have Joe Jones, your friend and independent repairman, or your car dealer's shop make necessary repairs, be sure to get an itemized bill for the work done. Be sure the car mileage is indicated on the bill every time you have the car serviced. Insist that the bill be properly dated. You never know when you may be asked to provide such evidence when you claim repairs under your warranty deed.

AVOID CLEANING SOLUTIONS THAT CAN HARM YOUR CAR!

Read carefully and follow the advice regarding proper inside and outside cleaning. Avoid cleansing solutions that will harm your car's finish. Take special precautions on plastic surfaces.

The selection of a good cleaner for your car upholstery will help preserve the new look long after you have had the car.

REMEDY FOR PARKING LOT BLUES!

Wherever there are small pit marks caused by the doors of other cars fill them in with a matching paint. Anywhere the paint is damaged fill it in. Corrosion can start even in a small area. Avoid the chain reaction—corrosion, depreciation, component failure.

RUST MAY WEAKEN YOUR CAR FRAME!

The Transportation Department's National Highway Traffic Safety Administration warns car owners and drivers that the chassis frames of old cars may be dangerously corroded. A survey by the agency's engineers shows that corrosion is not limited to any single make or model car.

Any car in use 5 years or longer that has been exposed to road splash containing concentrations of salt and dirt may have rust-weakened frames.

Heavy rust may weaken the inside surfaces of hollow frames although the exterior of the frames may show only normal surface rust. Road splash from wheels goes through drainage holes in the frames, and, if it does not drain, the splash containing salt and dirt may pocket within the frame and set up conditions for rust. Holes are in chassis frames to allow water to drain out of the frames and to provide air circulation. The safety agency recommends:

1. That owners and/or drivers of 1967 or earlier cars—which are operated on roads with concentrations of salt, calcium chloride, sand and moisture—examine (or have examined) the chassis frames for evidence of interior rusting.
2. That severely rusted frames be made safe by welding steel plates to the frames to bridge the corroded areas.
3. That owners and/or drivers periodically flush frames with a garden hose to reduce accumulation of corrosive material.
4. That owners of cars five or more years old furnish the agency with details of any severe rusting found in chassis frames.

If you find severe frame rusting, report it to the agency and include the make, model and year of the car. Send your report to:

National Highway Traffic Safety
   Administration
Office of Defects Investigation
Washington, D.C. 20590

FIND OUT HOW A CLEAN ENGINE CAN GIVE YOU BARGAINING POWER!

You may think your neighbor is a fanatic because he cleans his car engine each weekend. There is an advantage to a clean-looking engine. It gives you bargaining power come trade-in time when you show the dealer that your car engine looks like new. Any and all maintenance efforts you make benefit *you* in the long run.

HOW DO YOU RATE AUTO REPAIR SERVICE?

You buy a new car from the dealer who gives the best deal. When the car needs service or repair, you take it to the dealer's service department. After the work is done and you pay the bill, you learn something about the reliability of the dealer's service. Maybe excellent, maybe good, maybe bad. Maybe you've been had.

Virginia Knauer, Special Assistant to the President for Consumer Affairs, agrees with consumers that auto repair should not be by chance. "Too many consumers have paid for unnecessary repairs, and too many consumers have had repairs made with unsatisfactory results," she said. "Consumers should know the reliability of a dealer before—not after—repairs are made."

She has asked the major auto makers and the National Automobile Dealers Association to back a plan for a public rating system of auto service quality provided by dealers. She said an effective public rating system could increase competition in service and provide rewards for superior service. American Motors, Ford and NADA have indicated approval of the rating concept; General Motors and Chrysler Corporation have suggested other methods to improve auto service.

Mrs. Knauer also has asked the American Automobile Association, Center for Automobile Safety, Consumer Federation of America, Consumers Union, Transportation Department and individual members of NADA for specific recommendations and suggested additions to the proposed rating system.

If you have any comments about rating the service of auto dealers and how ratings might be made and compiled, write to:

Mrs. Virginia Knauer
Office of Consumer Affairs
New Executive Office Bldg.
Washington, D.C. 20506

HOW MUCH DOES IT COST TO OWN AND OPERATE YOUR CAR?

Do you know how much it really costs to own and operate your car? Probably not, but the

Federal Highway Administration has some estimates.

According to the revised edition of the agency's publication, "Cost of Operating an Automobile," you will spend about 13.55 cents a mile to drive and maintain a 1972 standard size car for 10 years, which is $13,552.95 for the estimated life of the car. If you have a 1972 compact, you will spend about 10.81 cents a mile, or $10,807.60 for using the car for 10 years. If you have a subcompact, you can count on spending 9.4 cents a mile, or $9,444.03 for using the subcompact for 10 years.

The purchase price is the first cost in the long line of costs that must be paid in operating your car during its approximate 100,000 mile, 10 year trip from the assembly line to the junkyard. Depreciation is by far the greatest single cost. Other costs for a 10-year period are: (1) $2,787 for some 7,350 gallons of gasoline; (2) $2,147 for maintenance and repairs; (3) $1,350 for insurance; (4) $1,800 for garaging, parking and tolls.

You may get a free copy of the report, "Cost Of Operating An Automobile," by writing to:
Federal Highway Administration
Transportation Dept.
Washington, D.C. 20590

Chapter 6

Tire Economy and Safety

DON'T NEGLECT YOUR TIRES!

Don't blame the manufacturer for poor mileage results if you neglect your tires. Use a good tire gauge to check "cool" tires every other week; at least once a month. Do not depend on air pump gauges at service stations.

IMPROPERLY INFLATED TIRES ARE DANGEROUS!

Over-inflated or under-inflated tires are extremely dangerous, especially when driving at high speeds. Tire pressure should not exceed the maximum indicated on the tires. Know how to determine your tires' complaints.

You must first realize that your tires do complain when they are improperly inflated. A hard ride means your tires are excessively inflated. A mushy ride and squealing when you turn corners means your tires are low and need a hose-to-valve resuscitation. Be alert to these signs of danger.

CAUSE AND EFFECT OF TIRE WEAR!

If any of the following conditions are allowed to continue over long periods, you increase the chances of a blowout and therefore endanger your safety:

1. Under-inflation causes rapid wear at tire shoulders.
2. Over-inflation causes rapid wear at the center of the tire.
3. Under-inflation or excessive speed causes cracked treads.
4. Excessive camber is the cause of wear on one side of the tire.
5. Incorrect toe causes feathered edges on tires.
6. Wheels that are unbalanced cause bald spots on tires.

HOW TO TELL WHETHER YOUR WHEELS ARE BALANCED AND PROPERLY ALIGNED!

You can't! There is no way you can tell whether your wheels are properly aligned by looking at them. So get them checked at least twice a year by a professional serviceman. Tires that are improperly aligned will show wear spots. A professional check will not only insure your safety; it will result in your getting better value for your tire dollar.

TIRE CODE LISTS

In 1971, the National Highway Traffic Safety Administration of the Transportation Department, assigned code letters to processors of retreaded tires and revised the list of code letters assigned to new tire manufacturers.

Lists of the tire codes were published in the Federal Register, and consumers were advised that they could obtain a reprint of the lists by sending 20 cents to the Superintendent of Documents. But they soon ran out of the lists and were unable to fill many requests by consumers.

Fortunately, consumers still interested in the lists may now obtain them free directly from the agency. Write to:
NHTSA
Tire Identification & Record Keeping
400 - 7th St., SW
Washington, D.C. 20590

SNOW AND TIRES

In many parts of the country, snow tires are an important consideration for winter driving. If you are thinking about using snow tires, studded tires or chains, here are some facts—compiled by the Transportation Department's National Traffic Highway Safety Administration.

Just as with conventional tires, it is important to select snow tires that fit your particular driving needs. If you will be driving in an area where snowfall is light, you will need tires designed for both snow and dry conditions. If, on the other hand, you will be driving in deep snow, you will need a tire with deep, open tread. For rainy conditions, the best tire is one with open channels in the tread to minimize water build-up.

Snow tires, like conventional tires, come in three basic types, classified according to their construction: bias-ply, bias-belted and radial. The kind you choose should depend on your driving requirements. However, a basic rule of thumb is to buy the same kind of snow tire as those on your front wheels. Mixing tire types can be extremely dangerous and should be avoided in both summer and winter driving.

Chains, in very snowy conditions especially, can make all the difference between getting out of your driveway and being snowed in. They provide excellent traction in hard-packed snow but severely limit driving speeds. The main drawback to chains, however, is that they are difficult to put on and must be taken off after each snow clears.

An alternative to snow tires and chains is the studded snow tire. However, because studs can damage roadways, these tires have been banned altogether in Louisiana, Mississippi, Minnesota, Utah and Hawaii. Their use has also been restricted in many other jurisdictions.

Studded tires have been proven to increase traction on ice. However, on snow, even deep snow, their performance rates about the same as regular snow tires. In rainy conditions, they provide less traction than ordinary snow tires.

The following are points to remember if you plan to buy studded tires:

Tires don't come with studs. They should be purchased at the store where you buy the tire and put in by an experienced serviceman.

Studded tires perform best with between 100 and 150 studs per tire. Over-studding will reduce traction and handling.

Before buying studded tires, make sure they are legal in your area. Also check to see how many months the highway regulations permit you to keep them on your car.

More information on snow and tires is available to consumers in the following publications: "Studded Tires—What Every Motorist Should Know" (free) and "Tires: Their Selection and Care" (65 cents for postage and handling). Write to:
Consumer Product Information
Washington, D.C. 20407

SKID DANGER

Just how much does rain increase the risk of skidding in your car? The Tire Industry Safety Council says the chances of skidding on wet pavement with tires having an average tread depth is 5 to 10 times as much as on a dry surface, and with bald tires the risk is 20 times as much.

The Council warns of another hazard caused by heavy rains and excess water on the road. A car traveling at too high a speed for road conditions can "hydroplane"—that is, the tires rise to the surface of the water, and there is complete loss of control.

DEALER INITIATES COMPARISON OF TIRE TESTS!

The Transportation Department's National Highway Traffic Safety Administration requires manufacturers to make all new car tires to meet minimum safety standards for strength, endurance, high-speed performance and bead unseating (tubeless tire's ability to withstand separation from the rim). The agency is currently evaluating responses to its proposal for a regulation that would require that comparative test information be made available to consumers.

Office of Consumer Affairs has reported that Market Tire Company, a tire dealer in the metropolitan Washington, D.C. area, is already making such data available. Market had Compliance Testing Inc. (a private testing firm) test samples of each of the 22 lines that Market sells, including 6 brand names and Market's private brand; the 22 lines comprise domestic and imported tires and the radial, belted and bias ply designs. The test results show how much various brands exceed the minimum standards.

The test results do not include comparisons for

traction and treadwear because the safety agency has not yet set standards for these two tire qualities. The agency is considering modification of its proposed Uniform Tire Quality Grading regulation to include traction and treadwear standards.

Market's test results (which do not cover all tire brands and lines being sold in the U.S.), as well as its booklet, "A Guide To Aid You In Tire Selection," are available, as long as the supply lasts, from:
Tire Tests
Consumer News
Office of Consumer Affairs
Washington, D.C. 20506

Office of Consumer Affairs does not vouch for the test results; it merely supports the idea of comparative data for consumers.

If you want to comment on the value of comparative tire performance information for consumers, write to:
Docket 25 Uniform Tire Quality Grading
National Highway Traffic
  Safety Administration
Transportation Dept.
Washington, D.C. 20590

BREAKING THE TIRE CODE!

The National Highway Traffic Safety Administration of the Transportation Department has assigned code letters to processors of retreaded tires and revised the list of code letters assigned to manufacturers of new tires. New tires are marked with a symbol "DOT" and a 2-letter code. Retreaded tires are marked with an "R" and a 3-letter code.

The agency adopted the code systems to facilitate tire recalls. The codes designate manufacturer or retreader and address. They do not contain any safety or performance information. By breaking the tire codes, a customer may satisfy his curiosity about which company really makes the tires sold by a national chain store, a franchised outlet or a local service station. Many manufacturers make tires that are sold under another brand name or under a store name or another company's name.

The Federal Register contains the lists of companies and codes. The agency does not require manufacturers, retreaders or retailers to make the lists available to consumers. And because of the lengths of the lists, they are not easy to reproduce. If you want a copy of the lists as published in the Federal Register, send your request and 20 cents for postage and handling to:

Superintendent of Documents
Government Printing Office
Washington, D.C. 20402

HOW TO SELECT AND CARE FOR YOUR TIRES—FREE GOVERNMENT BOOKLET!

This free booklet, "Tires, Their Selection and Care!" considers different types of tires, air pressure, safety and economy. Please include 65 cents for postage and handling and request Catalog No. S/N 0303-0681.
Superintendent of Documents
Government Printing Office
Washington, D.C. 20402

FREE BOOKLETS ON TIRES!

Now you can get free booklets on tires from a leading tire manufacturer. Find out how you can save money on the cost of tires; buying, selecting and caring for them. Why subject yourself to high costs and unsafe tires. Get the facts. Send your request to:
The Dayton Tire & Rubber Co.
P.O. Box 1026
Dayton, Ohio 45401
　　Attn: Public Relations Dept.

Chapter 7

Safety Equipment

GUIDELINES FOR BUYING CHILDREN'S CAR SEATS

If you purchased children's car seats prior to April 1, 1971, and want to know if they are safe, or if you are planning to purchase a child's seat now, you may want to read the National Highway Traffic Safety Administration's booklet, "What to Buy in Child Restraint Systems," which is available from:

Superintendent of Documents
Government Printing Office
Washington, D.C. 20402

The agency outlines the advantages of the various restraint systems, and lists points to consider in making a purchasing decision or in evaluating a previously purchased car seat:

1. Any seat that hooks over the seatback of the car is unsafe.
2. The child's seat must give protection from front and rear-end crashes, cushioning the

child and preventing him from being thrown.
3. The seat must give adequate protection against whiplash injury by having a head restraint.
4. The seat's restraint belts must be at least 1½ inches wide.
5. The child's upper body should be restrained by belts or impact pad.
6. Any seat constructed of easily bent, flimsy metal strapping, or padded only with thin sponge rubber is unsafe.
7. There must be no sharp or pointed hardware.
8. Do not use the wrong type of restraint system for the size of the child.

IMPROVED SEAT BELT SYSTEMS REQUIRED

The National Highway Traffic Safety Administration urges buyers of new cars to report any violation of new seat belt requirements or defective operation of seat belt systems. Under requirements of Federal Motor Vehicle Safety Standard No. 208, improved systems must be on all cars manufactured after January 1, 1972.

The standard requires:

Automatic-locking or emergency-locking retractors for lap belts in both front and rear outside seating positions.

All lap and shoulder belt combinations to have a 3-point design in which the shoulder belt attaches to the lap belt and releases when the lap belt is released.

A buzzer and flashing light warning system that reminds the driver and his front seat passenger about seat belts when the driver turns on the ignition and places the gear shift in a forward drive position.

Traffic Safety Administrator Douglas Toms urges drivers and occupants to wear available seat belts "because they provide the best protection currently available." A NHTSA survey indicates about 20 percent use seat belts and about 4 percent use shoulder belts. The agency estimates that thousands of lives could be saved annually if all car and truck occupants used seat belts.

To report a violation of the new seat-and-shoulder belt requirements or a defective operation of a system, write to:

National Highway Traffic Safety
   Administration
Dept. of Transportation
Washington, D.C. 20590

FREE AUTO SAFETY FACT SHEETS!

The National Highway Traffic Safety Administration has published a series of fact sheets about automobile safety:

1. "Safety Tips On The Purchase and Use Of Hydraulic Brake Fluids"
2. "Facts To Know About Importing A Foreign Car"
3. "The Hazards Of Mixing Tire Types"

4. "Safety Belts—A Step Closer To Automatic Crash-Survival"

Each fact sheet has a background summary of the subject and states some "do's" and "don't's" that consumers should follow for safety and/or legal reasons. The fact sheets are free from:
Consumer Product Information
Washington, D.C. 20407

FREE BOOKLET ON THE LAWS REQUIRING HELMETS AND EYE PROTECTION FOR MOTORCYCLISTS!

This booklet reviews requirements in the context of comparable requirements of the Uniform Vehicle Code. It reveals that state laws requiring use of such devices have generally been upheld by the courts, and briefly discusses the effect of not using helmets on the motorcyclist's right to receive compensation for his injuries. Please include 30 cents for postage and handling and ask for Catalog No. S/N 5003-00090. Write to:
Superintendent of Documents
Government Printing Office
Washington, D.C. 20402

FREE GUIDE HELPS YOU TEACH YOUR CHILDREN THE IMPORTANCE OF SAFETY BELTS!

This illustrated guide supplies information about why and how belts should be worn, some

reasons why they aren't worn, and some strategies for coping with resistance to safety belt usage. Makes learning about auto safety fun. Please include 40 cents for postage and handling. (Ask for Catalog No. S/N 5501-001770.)
Environmental Protection Agency
Superintendent of Documents
Government Printing Office
Washington, D.C. 20402

TEN COMMANDMENTS FOR DRIVERS, FREE!

Post these ten safe driving commandments on the dash, in your glove compartment or any other spot where they will be a daily reminder to drive safely. With only 10 percent of the population driving properly, you may need a reminder—ask for "Ten Commandments of Safe Driving" when writing to:
American Safety Council
154 Edgar Rd.
St. Louis, Mo. 63119

FREE QUESTIONS AND ANSWERS ON AUTOMOTIVE AIR BAGS!

Get informative answers to questions most often asked about automotive air bags. The answers are unbiased and explain the present state of the air bag. Questions and answers are continually updated to give you the latest facts. For your free copy of "Automotive Air Bags:

Questions and Answers," write to:
Allstate Insurance Company
Attn: Safety Director
Allstate Plaza
Northbrook, Ill. 60062

FREE GUIDE TO SAFE DRIVING
FROM ALLSTATE!

This valuable guide covers seat belts, air bags, bumpers, drunk driving, car theft, driver education, drivers' licenses, and the rising cost of auto insurance. Find out how you can make your driving safe. Write to Allstate and ask for "Driving: Our Good Hands are Working to Make it Better."
Allstate Insurance Company
Attn: Safety Director
Allstate Plaza
Northbrook, Il. 60062

FIND OUT WHAT YOU CAN DO TO GET
THE DRUNK DRIVER OFF THE ROAD!

This free guide takes an informative look at the drunk driver and what you can do to get him off the road. It covers the problem of drunk driving, charts on drinking, how you can help, laws, ways to stop the alcoholic driver and a digest of 16 standards of the National Highway Safety Act. Ask for "The Drunk Driver May Kill You," when writing to:

Allstate Insurance Company
Attn: Safety Director
Allstate Plaza
Northbrook, Il. 60062

FREE SAFETY BELT INSTRUCTIONAL BOOKLET!

You can obtain a programmed instructional text dealing with automobile safety belts. You answer questions about safety belts, then compare your answers to those in the pamphlet. Please include 20 cents for postage and handling and ask for Catalog No. S/N 5003-00077. Write to:

Superintendent of Documents
Government Printing Office
Washington, D.C. 20402

LATEST SAFETY STANDARD BOOKLET!

"Read Before Driving" briefly describes many of the safety standards being built into late model cars, observance of good safety practices, and what programs are now under consideration for the reduction of highway injuries and deaths to provide safer roads for all. A list of motor vehicle safety standards areas is included. Please include 15 cents for postage and handling and ask for Catalog No. 5003-0029.

Superintendent of Documents
Government Printing Office
Washington, D.C. 20402

Chapter 8

Buying Auto Supplies

FREE GUIDE TO THE SELECTION, USE AND MAINTENANCE OF ANTIFREEZE/COOLANT!

This free guide published by the General Services Administration gives the consumer and car owner valuable information about the selection, use and maintenance of antifreeze and coolant. Ask for "Antifreeze/Coolant"; please include 20 cents for postage and handling when writing to:
Consumer Product Information
Washington, D.C. 20407

EVERYTHING YOU SHOULD KNOW ABOUT AUTOMOBILE BATTERIES!

This booklet tells how to provide the routine care and maintenance which will keep an automobile battery operating dependably throughout its service life. It tells how a battery is made, how it operates, how it should be maintained, how to recognize the signs of battery failure,

and how to select a replacement battery. It also offers suggestions about how to get the most from your battery dollar! Please include 40 cents for postage and handling and ask for Catalog No. S/N 2200-0067.
Superintendent of Documents
Government Printing Office
Washington, D.C. 20402

ECONOMY IN DRIVING!

Whether or not a gasoline shortage develops, there are ways you can get more miles on each gallon—and save money. Among them, says the American Automobile Association, are these: Keep your car tuned up at all times—spark plugs, points, filters, carburetor; avoid jack-rabbit starts and quick stops; maintain a steady highway speed rather than alternately speeding up and slowing down; check your tires periodically to see that they are adequately inflated; use air conditioning sparingly.

FREE FACT SHEET ON AN AMAZING NEW INSTRUMENT FOR AUTO OWNERS!

A quality product for vehicle owners, Clino-W accurately measures those corners for you; tells you the rate of incline or decline on that hill you're going up; lets you know when your trailer is not resting level, and measures rate of acceleration and deceleration—car or boat, 4-wheel drive vehicle or truck. Fact sheet available from:

P & R Enterprises
4150 Maynard Ave.
Oakland, Ca. 94605

VALUABLE FACTS ON A BATTERY CORROSION KILLER!

This free fact sheet tells you about a battery corrosion killer you simply spray onto terminals and cables, wait sixty seconds and wipe off. Corrosion is gone—and its return retarded. Write to:
Grayco Industries, Inc.
Dept. FR-1/MW
336 Old Hook Rd.
Westwood, N.J. 07675

FREE FACT SHEET ON VACU-SHINE, THE DRY CLEAN AUTO CLOTH!

Vacu-Shine cleans and shines a car, bumper to bumper, in only five minutes. The chemicals are in the cloth. Use no soap, no water, no polish. Use day or night, summer and winter. Prevents dangerous misting on windshield. Valuable fact sheet is available free by writing to:
Grayco Industries, Inc.
Dept. FR-1/MW
336 Old Hook Rd.
Westwood, N.J. 07675

Chapter 9

Automobile Insurance

HOW TO SHOP FOR AUTO INSURANCE!

Shopping for auto insurance is the same as shopping for any other merchandise you buy. You want the best you can get for your money. Just as you go from store to store looking for the best price, you should check a number of insurance companies for the best buy.

Just because one insurance company agent says his is the best price available, don't you believe it until you have checked the prices of other insurance companies. You may be pleasantly surprised to find you can get a better price elsewhere.

HOW LIABILITY INSURANCE CAN SAVE YOU, YOUR HOME, YOUR SAVINGS AND YOUR SALARY!

Never, under any circumstance, get behind the wheel of your car unless you are covered with liability insurance. "Bodily injury" and "property damage liability," as specified under liability insurance, covers you if someone is injured or property is damaged, and you are legally liable. Liability insurance is a must for every driver!

Liability insurance is not the area you should be looking at for savings. Get all the liability insurance you can afford. Remember this—you are liable for amounts over the figure you are covered for in your policy. Don't jeopardize your future.

HERE'S HOW A SMALL AMOUNT CAN GIVE YOU MORE COVERAGE ON PROPERTY DAMAGE!

Rates vary from one company to another, so one cannot be exact about amounts of coverage. Here is a general idea of what you can get for a couple of dollars more:

$10/20,000   Premium—$100
$25/50,000   Premium—$115
$100/300,000 Premium—$135

In many states 10/20/5 is the minimum policy limit. What it means is $10,000 for one person, $20,000 for bodily injury in any given accident and $5,000 in property damage.

CAN YOU SAVE ON SINGLE LIMIT POLICIES?

As a rule there is not a big savings under a single limit policy, but any savings is still money in your pocket. Ask your insurance agent about a single limit policy.

FIND OUT HOW YOU CAN SAVE MONEY ON COLLISION INSURANCE!

Collision insurance comes with all kinds of deductibles. This is one area where you can bring the cost of your insurance down. Ask your insurance agent to explain deductibles to you.

DON'T CARRY COLLISION INSURANCE ON AN OLDER CAR!

Most compact cars and foreign imports are worth, on an average, $700 after three years, and almost any car has depreciated enough after five years to make collision insurance unnecessary. Here is one way you can save on the cost of auto insurance. Put the money you would be paying in premiums for collision insurance on an older car in the bank. After five years you will enjoy a sizeable savings plus interest.

GET AS MUCH MEDICAL COVERAGE AS YOU CAN AFFORD!

Med Pay means money immediately in the case of injury to you or any of your passengers. You can also get more coverage for just a few dollars more. A fact to keep in mind is that Med Pay is the cheapest and most valuable coverage available. Don't be among the many who overlook this important coverage.

FIND OUT IF COMPREHENSIVE INSURANCE IS VALUABLE TO YOU!

Unless you live in a high-theft area, it isn't necessary to carry comprehensive insurance. Premiums for comprehensive run high for high-theft areas. If you can afford to carry comprehensive, do so. It is still a lot cheaper than buying a new car should yours be stolen.

WHAT IS UNINSURED MOTORIST COVERAGE—AND HOW WORTHWHILE IS IT?

It is *very* worthwhile and it is exceptionally inexpensive. If you are hit by an uninsured or hit-and-run driver, your company will pay the bills up to the limit of your policy.

HOW YOU CAN SAVE MONEY ON AUTO INSURANCE COVERAGE FOR YOUR CHILDREN!

If you have children who are driving and if they have successfully completed a recognized driver education course, you can save on the amount of insurance coverage for each child who completes the course.

If you have children of driving age who are nonresident students, you can obtain a discount on your insurance. However, in most cases, the school your children attend must be at least 100 miles from where the family car is garaged.

FIND OUT HOW THE SAFE DRIVER PLAN CAN SAVE YOU UP TO 20 PERCENT IN PREMIUMS!

If each member of your family who drives the car has never had an accident and if each member has not been convicted of a serious driving violation in the past three years, you are eligible for a discount under the safe driver plan.

SAVE MONEY—INSURE TWO!

If you own two or more cars and if you insure both or all with the same company, you will receive a discount of about 15 percent.

A PACKAGE DEAL SAVES YOU MONEY!

If you buy a special auto insurance policy that combines liability, medical, collision and comprehensive coverage, you can obtain a savings over what you would have to pay for each item individually.

HERE'S HOW YOU CAN SAVE IF YOU ARE 16-25! ASK ABOUT THE "NEW CLASS PLAN"!

If you are 16-25, before you purchase insurance, ask the agent if he offers the "New Class Plan." Under this plan you are eligible for a premium decrease for every violation-free birthday. This plan can make a large difference in the amount you pay as you approach 25.

WHAT IS NO-FAULT INSURANCE COVERAGE!

No-fault insurance compensates you for any loss or cost which results from an accident. There is no need to find out which driver caused the accident. Pure no-fault denies the right of suit to obtain more extensive damages. Most plans in effect are modified no-fault plans allowing for suit if damages pass a given amount. Loss of income provisions and medical payments begin immediately.

FREE SHOPPER'S GUIDE TO AUTOMOBILE INSURANCE!

Prepared by the Pennsylvania Insurance Department, this free shopper's guide includes some key premium comparisons for beginning your search for the best automobile insurance bargain. An excellent way to acquaint yourself with insurance lingo and learn how to shop for insurance bargains. Send your request to:
Pennsylvania Insurance Department
Harrisburg, Pa.

BEFORE YOU BUY MAIL ORDER INSURANCE, BE AWARE OF THE COMMON PITFALLS!

This free guide, "Pitfalls In Mail Order Insurance," helps you become aware of the many common pitfalls in mail order insurance. Before you buy any insurance, shop around for the best

buy available. Ask for your free guide.
Federal Trade Commission
6th St. & Pennsylvania Ave., NW
Washington, D.C. 20580

Chapter 10

Save On Financing

HERE'S HOW TO GET *UNDERSTANDABLE* FINANCING INFORMATION!

It is much easier to get a straight answer to your financing questions today than it was a few years ago. If you know what questions to ask you can get the best financing deal available. Most reputable finance companies offer information even if you don't ask. Truth-in-lending laws make it a requirement for lenders to reveal certain financing facts not available to the general public a few years ago. So before you look for financing, know what questions will help you get a good financing deal.

HERE'S HOW YOU CAN GET A GOOD FINANCING DEAL!

Shop around—find out what several car dealers are offering and compare their offers.

And only talk about financing when you have received firm quotes on the price of the car you select. Do not talk about a trade-in until you have received the best cash-price quote; then talk about financing and trade-in.

DON'T TRY TO REMEMBER ALL THE FACTS!

Unless you are familiar with financial terms, it is senseless to try to remember all the facts as they are given to you from dealers, commercial banks, credit unions, insurance companies, etc. *Write the facts down.* Don't try to compare the facts as you get them. Go home, have a cup of coffee and compare the facts against each other.

ASK THE DEALER ABOUT THE TRUE ANNUAL INTEREST RATE! KNOWING WILL SAVE YOU MONEY!

Find out what the true *annual percentage interest rate* is. The dealer must provide this information. Get the true rate in terms of a specific loan time period. The true annual rate is usually double the 5 to 8 percent he first quoted.

Ask the dealer to tell you in dollars and cents what the interest charge will be. Ask him to explain it in terms of a *usable* amount of money borrowed for a given period of time. Interest does not mean the same thing in discounted and add-on loans.

DEALER FINANCING IS NOT THE ONLY SOURCE OF BORROWED MONEY! CHECK OUT ANY AND ALL OTHER POSSIBILITIES!

The dealer is not always the top source. Before you settle on financing, examine other possibilities such as commercial banks, credit unions, insurance companies and the bank where you save. Ask each source to give you both dollar and true annual percentage costs for the same amount of money for the same amount of time. Use your phone to obtain information.

YOU CAN SAVE MONEY BY BORROWING FROM YOUR OWN SAVINGS ACCOUNT!

If you have ample funds in your savings account, you might save a good amount by borrowing from yourself. First find out what it would cost (in dollars) to float a loan at a commercial bank or other lending institution. Compare how much interest you would lose by taking it out of your savings account and how much interest you would pay if you borrowed through a conventional auto-financing plan. Ask the bank to put it in dollars and cents for you; it makes for an easier comparison.

NOT EVERY COMMERCIAL BANK OFFERS THE SAME FINANCING! CHECK SEVERAL OF THEM OUT FOR A BETTER FINANCING DEAL!

Do not assume that every commercial bank will

offer you the same financing. Check out the banks in your area, one at a time, then compare for the best possible financing available.

CREDIT UNIONS SOMETIMES OFFER VERY GOOD RATES!

If you are a member of a credit union, check out their auto financing plans. Most credit unions offer very good rates. Take advantage of your membership in a credit union.

WHAT ABOUT INSURANCE COMPANIES? CHECK OUT THEIR FINANCING DEALS!

Many insurance companies specializing in auto liability insurance are now offering auto financing, and their rates are competitive with commercial banks. Check every possible means of auto financing before you decide.

FREE FAIR CREDIT GUIDE FOR CONSUMERS!

"Know Your Rights Under The Fair Credit Reporting Act: A Checklist for Consumers" is a must for every potential new car buyer. Please include 10 cents for postage and handling and ask for Stock No. 1800-0138. Published by the Fededal Trade Commission, the guide is available from:

Superintendent of Documents
Government Printing Office
Washington, D.C. 20402

FREE GUIDE FOR CONSUMERS ON THE TRUTH-IN-LENDING LAWS!

Dealers are required by law to state certain financing truths. Some dealers, however, wait for you to ask. "Credit Terms in Common Use Under Truth-in-Lending" will help you ask the right questions and perhaps save you from a rough financing deal. Ask for it by title from:
Federal Trade Commission
6th St. & Pennsylvania Ave., NW
Washington, D.C. 20580

VALUABLE TRUTH-IN-LENDING ILLUSTRATIONS! AVAILABLE IN FULL-COLOR OR BLACK-AND-WHITE!

Now you can get these valuable truth-in-lending illustrations in both full-color and black-and-white. They will be your guide to a fair deal. If you don't know what questions to ask, you may be taken. Ask for "Truth-in-Lending Illustrations" and specify color or black-and-white.
Federal Trade Commission
6th St. and Pennsylvania Ave., NW
Washington, D.C. 20580

Chapter 11

The Internal Revenue Service Can Help You

FREE REPORT ON USE TAX ON TRUCKS, TRUCK-TRACTORS AND BUSES

Report No. 349 is especially important to tens of millions of motorists now, in light of the added millions of recreational vehicles that are being sold each year—not to mention the many van-type trucks being used for hauling and for personal transportation. To see if this report applies to you and what you may own, all you have to do is call, write or visit your local IRS office and ask for a free copy of Publication No. 349.

FREE IRS REPORT THAT MAY MEAN REFUNDS FOR YOU!

Federal Fuel Tax Credit or Refund for Non-Highway and Transit Users, Publication No. 378, may save you money. Under certain circumstances you may be eligible for federal fuel tax credits or refunds; find out what it is all about.

Just write, call or visit your local IRS office and ask for your free copy of Publication No.

378. Read it carefully when you do get it and see if it can mean any refunds for you.

FREE REPORT FROM IRS ABOUT WHAT TRAVEL AND ENTERTAINMENT EXPENSES YOU ARE ENTITLED TO DEDUCT FROM YOUR INCOME TAXES!

In this day and age, when so much entertaining requires using, owning and renting a car and other vehicles, it is very important to know what travel, entertainment and gift expenses are deductible and how you can keep the kind of records IRS requires in order to justify these tax deductions.

Why guess, when you can get all the information in Publication No. 463, "Travel, Entertainment and Gift Expenses," by telephoning, visiting or writing your local IRS office.

FREE GUIDE TO EXCISE TAXES!

So many high excise taxes are added on to the price of all types of vehicles by the manufacturers (and to the price of supplies and parts for vehicles). All we see is the final price. Publication No. 510 actually tells you all about excise taxes (especially on big ticket vehicle prices) and how much we are paying. Some of these taxes may be deductible from your income taxes as a business expense, so the least you should do is call, write or visit your local IRS office and ask for Publication No. 510.

EXCISE TAX INFORMATION ON IMPORTED FOREIGN-MADE VEHICLES

So many millions of foreign vehicles of all kinds are being bought by Americans each year that it may come as a surprise that there are excise taxes and the like on such vehicles.

If you are an owner of a foreign-made vehicle, or are contemplating buying one, visit, write or call your local IRS office and ask for "Excise Tax Information on Imported Foreign-Made Automobiles," Publication No. 707. It is free for the asking, so make yourself aware of just what is involved in such a purchase, cost-wise.

CAN YOU DEDUCT DEPRECIATION ON YOUR VEHICLE(S)?

"Sales and Other Dispositions of Depreciable Property" tells you about autos, trucks, delivery vehicles and vehicles of all kinds used in business or to make money or for both business and pleasure.

What happens when you get ready to sell a car or a truck or any other vehicle, as far as depreciation rates go on your income tax? Publication No. 511 answers all of these questions for you, and it is free to you if you just call, visit or write your local IRS office.

FREE TAX INFORMATION GUIDE ON MOVING EXPENSES

Millions of people are now using their cars and

assorted vehicles and trailers of all types to help them move. If you do your own moving, whether job related or not, how much of the cost can you deduct? Well, many costs are deductible, but many are not. And there's only one way to find out for sure.

Call, write or visit your local IRS Office and ask for Publication No. 521, "Tax Information On Moving Expenses." It's free, and you'll have all of the information right in front of you. Don't lose out because you don't know for sure!

HOW MANY DIFFERENT DEDUCTIONS ARE THERE FOR VEHICLE OWNERS?

Internal Revenue has prepared a publication called "Other Miscellaneous Deductions" (No. 529) which includes all sorts of deductions for vehicles used in different type situations. As a car or truck owner, or as the owner of any type of vehicle, it would be an excellent idea for you to know what you may be entitled to deduct that you are not already deducting! Just write, visit or call your local IRS office for your free copy.

FREE PUBLICATION—TAX INFORMATION ON REPAIRS, REPLACEMENTS AND IMPROVEMENTS!

Every vehicle owner (of any type vehicle) should know what the tax situation is with regard to repairs, replacements and improvements. Although designed really for those making building improvements of all types, this IRS guide can also be extremely helpful (and profitable) to vehicle owners—especially in light of today's expensive repair and replacement costs of vehicles of any and all types. Call, write or visit your local IRS office and ask for Publication No. 540.

INTEREST PAID ON YOUR VEHICLE
PAYMENTS MAY BE DEDUCTIBLE!

What interest expenses do you have in connection with any vehicle (of any type) that you own? Are you entitled to deduct those interest amounts on your income tax return? If so, what proof do you need to back up the deduction of the amount of interest you pay on your vehicle? All of these questions and more are answered in a fascinating IRS publication (No. 545), "Income Tax Deduction For Interest Expenses." Know what your rights and deductions are. Write, visit or telephone your local IRS office for your free copy.

SECTION TWO

CONSUMER PROTECTION

Chapter 12

Government Specifications For Your Vehicle

U.S. GENERAL SERVICES ADMINISTRATION FEDERAL SPECIFICATIONS FOR ANTIFREEZE!

Now for the first time you can find out what specs your government requires for the antifreeze it buys. Ask for 0-A-00548 (and include 10 cents for postage and handling). The specs also include such valuable consumer buying information as the brand name equivalent of items purchased by GSA under federal specs, name and address of the manufacturer, model numbers and much more. Write to:
GSA Specification Sales
Bldg. 197
Washington Navy Yard
Washington, D.C. 20407

FEDERAL SPECIFICATIONS FOR BATTERIES!

You can find out what specs your government requires for the batteries it buys. Ask for W-B-131, (and include 10 cents for postage and handling). The specs also include such valuable consumer buying information as the brand name equivalent of items purchased by GSA under federal specs, name and address of the manufacturer, model numbers and much more. Write to:
GSA Specification Sales
Bldg. 197
Washington Navy Yard
Washington, D.C. 20407

FEDERAL SPECIFICATIONS FOR BRAKE FLUID!

Find out what the government requires in the brake fluid it buys. Ask for VV-B-680 (and include 15 cents for postage and handling). The specs also include such buying information as the brand name equivalent of items purchased by GSA under federal specs, name and address of the manufacturer, model numbers and much more. Write to:
GSA Specification Sales
Bldg. 197
Washington Navy Yard
Washington, D.C. 20407

U.S. GENERAL SERVICES ADMINISTRATION FEDERAL SPECIFICATIONS FOR CAR POLISH!

Government specs for car polish are now available. Ask for P-P-546 (and include 10 cents for postage and handling). The specs also include such valuable consumer buying information as the brand name equivalent of items purchased by GSA under federal specs, name and address of the manufacturer, model numbers and much more. Write to:

GSA Specification Sales
Bldg. 197
Washington Navy Yard
Washington, D.C. 20407

FEDERAL SPECIFICATIONS FOR SPARK PLUGS!

You can find out what specs your government requires for the spark plugs it buys. Ask for W-S-506 (and include 15 cents for postage and handling). The specs also include such information as the brand name equivalent of items purchased by GSA under federal specs, name and address of the manufacturer, model numbers and much more. Write to:

GSA Specification Sales
Bldg. 197
Washington Navy Yard
Washington, D.C. 20407

U.S. GENERAL SERVICES ADMINISTRATION FEDERAL SPECIFICATIONS FOR TIRE CHAINS!

What does the government require in the tire chains it buys. Ask for RR-C-00281 and please include 15 cents for postage and handling. The specs also include such valuable consumer buying information as the brand name and equivalent of items purchased by GSA under federal specs, name and address of the manufacturer, model numbers and much more.

GSA Specification Sales
Bldg. 197
Washington Navy Yard
Washington, D.C. 20407

FEDERAL SPECIFICATIONS FOR TIRES ON PASSENGER CARS AND LIGHT TRUCKS!

For the first time you can find out what specs your government requires for the tires it buys. Ask for ZZ-T-00381. The specs also include such valuable consumer buying information as the brand name equivalent of items purchased by GSA under federal specs, name and address of the manufacturer, model numbers and much more. Write to:

GSA Specification Sales
Bldg. 197
Washington Navy Yard
Washington, D.C. 20407

U.S. GENERAL SERVICES ADMINISTRATION FEDERAL SPECIFICATIONS FOR WINDSHIELD ICE SCRAPER AND SQUEEGEE!

Now for the first time you can find out what specs your government requires for the windshield ice scraper and squeegee it buys. Ask for GGG-S-001333. The specs also include such valuable consumer buying information as the brand name equivalent of items purchased by GSA under federal specs, name and address of the manufacturer, model numbers and much more.

GSA Specification Sales
Bldg. 197
Washington Navy Yard
Washington, D.C. 20407

FEDERAL SPECIFICATIONS FOR SEDANS!

Find out what specs your government requires for the sedans it buys. Ask for KKK-A-00811. The specs also include such valuable consumer buying information as the brand name equivalent of items purchased by GSA under federal specs, name and address of the manufacturer, model numbers and much more.

GSA Specification Sales
Bldg. 197
Washington Navy Yard
Washington, D.C. 20407

U.S. GENERAL SERVICES ADMINISTRATION FEDERAL SPECIFICATIONS FOR STATION WAGONS!

Now for the first time you can find out what specs your government requires for the station wagons it buys. Ask for KKK-A-00850. The specs also include such valuable consumer buying information as the brand name equivalent of items purchased by GSA under federal specs, name and address of the manufacturer, model numbers and much more. Write to:

GSA Specification Sales
Bldg. 197
Washington Navy Yard
Washington, D.C. 20407

FEDERAL SPECIFICATIONS FOR AUTO WAX!

You can find out what specs your government requires for the auto wax it buys. Ask for P-W-120 (and include 10 cents for postage and handling). The specs also include such valuable consumer buying information as the brand name equivalent of items purchased by GSA under federal specs, name and address of the manufacturer, model numbers and much more. Write to:

GSA Specification Sales
Bldg. 197
Washington Navy Yard
Washington, D.C. 20407

FEDERAL SPECIFICATIONS FOR WINDSHIELD WIPER BLADES!

For the first time you can find out what specs your government requires for the windshield wiper blades it buys. Ask for RR-A-1147 (and include 15 cents for postage and handling). The specs also include such valuable consumer buying information as the brand name equivalent of items purchased by GSA under federal specs, name and address of the manufacturer, model numbers and much more.

GSA Specification Sales
Bldg. 197
Washington Navy Yard
Washington, D.C. 20407

Chapter 13

Advice From The Federal Trade Commission

FREE ECONOMIC REPORT ON THE USE OF GAMES OF CHANCE IN GASOLINE RETAILING

Before the so-called shortage of gasoline was announced your local gas station had all sorts of games to lure you into the station. Your Federal Trade Commission has studied the results of all of these games and what the end result was as far as increasing the cost of gasoline. Write to the following address for a very interesting and in depth report on the cost of "free games":
Consumer Education Division
Bureau of Consumer Protection
Federal Trade Commission
Washington, D.C. 20580

FREE REPORT ON WHY THERE IS NO COMPETITION IN THE "FREE-ENTERPRISE" OIL INDUSTRY IN AMERICA!

How can one industry create overnight a gasoline and oil shortage? Is this merely a manufac-

tured shortage? This report tells you definitely and completely why the big oil companies can do anything they want to—and charge us all they want, too! For your free copy of "Report on Anticompetitive Practices In The Marketing of Gasoline," write to:
Consumer Education Division
Bureau of Consumer Protection
Federal Trade Commission
Washington, D.C. 20580

NOW YOU CAN GUARD AGAINST PHONY ADS FOR CARS, REPAIRS, PARTS!

This latest report from your Federal Trade Commission tells you in detail how to guard against (and spot) phony ads for all sorts of products and services. The report offers easy to use and easy to remember rules to follow before you spend your hard-earned money. No family should be without this report. For your free copy of "How To Guard Against Phony Ads," write to:
Consumer Education Division
Bureau of Consumer Protection
Federal Trade Commission
Washington, D.C. 20580

HOW TO PROTECT YOURSELF WHEN YOU BUY AUTO INSURANCE BY MAIL!

Millions of Americans buy their auto insurance by mail from mail order auto insurance com-

panies. Now the Federal Trade Commission has published guides for the mail order insurance industry to follow, to protect you, the consumer. If you buy, or are considering buying any type of insurance by mail, be sure you have these guides on hand, because these are the same guides that rule the insurance companies that sell by mail. For your free copies of "Guides For The Mail Order Insurance Industry," write to:
Consumer Education Division
Bureau of Consumer Protection
Federal Trade Commission
Washington, D.C. 20580

HOW THE FTC PROTECTS TIRE BUYERS

With tire prices at an all time high, buying one or more tires for your car can be expensive —and puzzling, to say the least, with all the claims being made for all different types of tires. Now the FTC has released a new report, "Tire Advertising and Labeling Guides." These guides are the ones that tire manufacturers and sellers must read and follow when they make and sell tires to the public. You should also know what the FTC requires of makers and sellers of tires, especially in their advertising. For your free guides write to:
Consumer Education Division
Bureau of Consumer Protection
Federal Trade Commission
Washington, D.C. 20580

AN FTC ECONOMIC REPORT ON THE MANUFACTURE AND DISTRIBUTION OF AUTO TIRES

Is there any competition among tire manufacturers and sellers? Why are the prices of all the brands so much alike? How many different companies do the major tire manufacturers actually make tires for? Here, for the first time, is an in-depth report on the tire manufacturing and distributing industry and what it means to you as the buyer of tires. For your free economic report, ask for "The Manufacture and Distribution of Tires."

Consumer Education Division
Bureau of Consumer Protection
Federal Trade Commission
Washington, D.C. 20580

A NEW FTC REPORT TO CONSUMERS AND MANUFACTURERS

"Rules of The Tire and Tube Repair Material Industry" covers a new set of industry guides that the FTC issues to govern the tire and tube repair materials industry.

So, when you go out to buy recapped tires or repaired tubes, or tube and tire repair kits, you are protected. But you will be more protected if you, yourself, write for and read the industry guides. Then you will know what to look for—and what to look out for. For your free copy, write to:

Consumer Education Division
Bureau of Consumer Protection
Federal Trade Commission
Washington, D.C. 20580

HERE ARE THE RULES THAT MUST BE FOLLOWED BY THE REBUILT, RECONDITIONED AND OTHER USED AUTO PARTS SELLERS!

Millions of vehicle owners have turned to using rebuilt, reconditioned and used parts of all types in order to keep repair costs down. Now the FTC has published guides for these people to follow with regard to the quality of parts sold and dealing with the public. It would be a good idea for all consumers to have these guides, too. Know what standards the government expects from this industry. For your free guides, write to:

Consumer Education Division
Bureau of Consumer Protection
Federal Trade Commission
Washington, D.C. 20580

HERE ARE THE FTC TRADE REGULATION RULES GOVERNING BATTERIES!

The FTC has issued trade regulation rules covering warranties and guarantees of batteries, including the use of such terms as "leakproof" and "guaranteed leakproof". Buying the right battery

can not only save you money, but it can also save you a lot of time and trouble during the lifetime of the battery in your vehicle. Find out for yourself what deceptive practices and guarantees to avoid when you shop for and buy a battery. For your free copy of the trade rules governing batteries, write to:
Consumer Education Division
Bureau of Consumer Protection
Federal Trade Commission
Washington, D.C. 20580

FREE CONSUMER EDUCATION GUIDE: HOW TO GUARD YOURSELF AGAINST DEBT COLLECTION DECEPTIONS!

Guidelines prepared by the FTC for use by industry to clarify specific industry problems and illuminate types of illegalities. Consumers will find these guidelines an invaluable source of information on protection against debt collection deceptions. Ask for "Guides Against Debt Collection Deceptions." Write to:
Federal Trade Commission
6th St. & Pennsylvania Ave., NW
Washington, D.C. 20580

FREE GUIDE TELLS HOW TO PREPARE AND PRESENT YOUR VIEWS TO THE FTC!

An invaluable guide to preparing and presenting your views at FTC consumer hearings. An excellent guide for the consumer interested in

subjects before the FTC. Ask for your free copy of "How To Prepare And Present Your Views At FTC Hearings."
Federal Trade Commission
6th St. & Pennsylvania Ave., NW
Washington, D.C. 20580

FREE SUBSCRIPTION TO *CONSUMER ALERT!*

Consumer Alert is a monthly summary of FTC actions of special interest to consumers. Now you can get a free subscription to this valuable publication by requesting it from:
Federal Trade Commission
6th St. & Pennsylvania Ave., NW
Washington, D.C. 20580

Chapter 14

How To Protect Yourself Against Auto Fire and Theft

ADDED PROTECTION AGAINST THEFT!
The DD Auto Alarm can be used as a triggering device for door burglar alarms. Put one under the hood and one in the trunk space. Protect your car from theft. Ask for more information on the DD Auto Alarm and other auto alarm systems from:
Watch Dog Alarm Co.
492 E. Main St.
Williamsburg, Ohio 45176

VALUABLE FACTS ABOUT AUTO
FIRE EXTINGUISHERS!
Now you can protect yourself, your passengers and your car from fire through a device that is a dry chemical substance that will put out an auto fire instantly when directed at the base of the flames. Get the facts on the auto fire extinguisher that can best serve you. Write to:

Watch Dog Alarm Co.
492 E. Main St.
Williamsburg, Ohio 45176

STOP AUTO THEFT! FREE FACT SHEET
ON THE ELECTRONIC PROTECTOR—
AUTO GUARD!

At last there is a truly positive protection against master keys, jumping starters, hot wiring the ignition and other common theft techniques. Easily installed by anyone, Auto Guard provides maximum security against theft. For more information on the Auto Guard write to:

Warnax Alarm Co.
Public Relations Dept.
Box 2066
Ventor, N.J. 08406

FREE FACT SHEET ON THE SECURITY
AUTO EXTINGUISHER

Now you can get performance and versatility with this dry-chemical extinguisher. The greatest advancement ever in fire fighting equipment is only 3 lbs.—and it puts out fires in three seconds. Refilling saves you money. Write for your free fact sheet from:

Warnax Alarm Co.
Public Relations Dept.
Box 2066
Ventor, N.J. 08406

SELF-PROTECTION SPRAY FOR YOUR GLOVE COMPARTMENT!

If you have to travel at night or in high-crime areas you should protect yourself from thieves and molesters. Compact for your glove compartment, the sprayer fits neatly in the palm of your hand. One burst immediately disables an attacker. It does not cause permanent injury. Free fact sheet available from:

Grayco Chemical Corp.
Dept. FR-2/MW
336 Old Hook Rd.
Westwood, N.J. 07675

Chapter 15

Ralph Nader and The Center For Auto Safety Reports

We are very grateful to The Center For Auto Safety and to Ralph Nader for granting us permission to make all of their reports, press releases, investigations and recommendations available to the American people. Each report is available for only the cost of photocopying, postage and handling. The Center is a non-profit organization.

Please request each report by complete description and date, and allow approximately four weeks for delivery as the center is often swamped with requests.

As you can see from the many listings in this chapter, the reports, releases, warnings and recommendations cover many different automotive subjects, including the most important subject of all, auto safety.

Read all of the listings carefully to see which ones can save you money and help you protect yourself and your family.

For ordering any of the materials included in this chapter, write to:
Center for Auto Safety
1223 Dupont Circle Bldg.
Washington, D.C. 20036

FREE GUIDE TELLS HOW TO ESTABLISH YOUR OWN LOCAL AUTO COMPLAINT ORGANIZATION!

Now you and other concerned members of your community can establish a local auto complaint organization to deal with fraudulent practices in auto purchasing, repairs, warranties and guarantees. Ask for your free guide, entitled "A Nader Guide for Establishing Local Auto Complaint Organizations".

CENTER RELEASE REVIEWS BOOKLET, "GUIDE TO SOURCES OF INFORMATION ON AUTO DEFECTS"

The Center has compiled a new booklet entitled "Guide to Sources of Information on Auto Defects." The guide was prepared in response to requests from attorneys and researchers interested in auto defects and recall campaigns. This release, dated July 13, 1972, is a brief summary of the contents of that booklet and provides information on obtaining copies. Please include 20 cents to cover mailing and copying cost.

LOOPHOLES IN FEDERAL MOTOR VEHICLE SAFETY STANDARDS!

The Center for Auto Safety, on August 17, 1973, formally requested the new head of the National Highway Traffic Safety Administration to close a series of loopholes in federal motor vehicle safety standards allowing manufacturers of light trucks, motor homes and other vehicles to sell their units to the public even though they lack many of the critical safety features which are required on all passenger cars. Please include 20 cents to cover photocopying, handling and postage.

CENTER RECOMMENDATIONS FOR AMENDMENTS, DELETIONS AND ADDITIONS TO MOTOR VEHICLE SAFETY STANDARDS!

On January 4, 1973, the Center sent the National Highway Traffic Safety Administration recommendations for amendments, deletions and additions to the proposed regulations governing the issuance of temporary exemptions from motor vehicle safety standards. Please include 30 cents to cover the cost of photocopying, handling and postage.

CENTER FOR AUTO SAFETY PETITION TO AMEND DEFECT REPORTS!

The purpose of this petition is to amend Part 573, Defect Reports, so that manufacturers would be required to report to the Department of Transportation the vehicle identification numbers (VIN) of the vehicles included in safety defect recall campaigns. This would help owners whose names have not been included on the notification mailing list. Please include 30 cents to cover the cost of photocopying the petition, handling and postage.

CENTER COMMENTS ON PROPOSED HIGHWAY SAFETY PROGRAM STANDARDS

Comments submitted to the National Highway Traffic Safety Administration on January 2, 1973 urged each state to require specific standards with regard to traffic safety education. Please include 30 cents to cover the cost of photocopying, handling and postage.

CENTER RESPONDS TO AD HOC COMMITTEE REPORT ON REGULATORY EFFECTS ON THE COSTS OF AUTOMOTIVE TRANSPORTATION

This report is a Nixon Administration assessment of technologies for obtaining clean air by reducing automotive emissions and for providing safety in automotive transportation, in terms of costs and benefits.

The Center responds to the sections of the report of the Ad Hoc Committee on Regulatory Effects on the Costs of Automotive Transportation which deal with auto safety. Please include 40 cents to cover the cost of photocopying, handling and postage.

CENTER ASKS THAT MATERIALS INDICATED IN AD HOC FINAL REPORT BE MADE AVAILABLE FOR PUBLIC INSPECTION!

In a letter to the Committee on March 22, 1972, the Center asks that materials be made available for public inspection. These materials include meeting transcripts, papers, presentations, replies to questionnaires, independent calculations and assessments and other sources which the preface of the report of the Ad Hoc Committee indicates were taken into account by the Committee in the course of its study. Please include 20 cents to cover the cost of photocopying, handling and postage.

PETITION FILED WITH THE FEDERAL TRADE COMMISSION TO DECLARE STP OIL TREATMENT A WORTHLESS PRODUCT!

This release dated May 25, 1973 is a summary of the petition filed with the Federal Trade Commission to declare STP Oil Treatment a worthless product, and asking the Commission to order STP Corporation to return to purchasers of the product funds obtained through unfair and deceptive advertising. Please include 30 cents to cover mailing and copying costs.

A REPORT ON FUEL SYSTEM INTEGRITY!

In this letter to the National Highway Traffic Safety Administration dated October 3, 1972, the Center stresses the need to upgrade Standard 301, Fuel System Integrity. As a result of vulnerable vehicle fuel system components automobiles continue to have the problem of vehicle fires. This letter is a report on fuel system components. Please include 30 cents to cover photocopying, handling and postage.

RELEASE ON AIR CUSHIONS AND MAXIMUM SAFETY SEAT BELTS!

In this letter to Mr. Edward N. Cole, President of General Motors Corporation, the Center for Auto Safety questions Mr. Cole's concept of less protective seat belts in autos using air cushion support. The Center also gives the basis for their firm support of air cushions. This letter of July 12, 1973 gives valuable facts on the air cushion concept. Please include 30 cents to cover the cost of photocopying, handling and postage.

CHILD AND INFANT CAR SAFETY SEATS AND RENTAL CARS

The Center for Auto Safety on June 13, 1973 challenged six of the nation's largest auto renting firms to make child and infant car safety seats available at all of their rental outlets. The Center's letter stated that failure to provide such facilities "unnecessarily endangers the lives of the thousands of small children who ride in your rental cars each year." To obtain a copy of this release, please include 10 cents to cover photocopying, handling and postage.

RECOMMENDATIONS ON SEAT BELT SYSTEMS IN NEW AUTOMOBILES!

The Center made recommendations to the National Highway Traffic Safety Administration on November 15, 1972, regarding seat belt systems in new automobiles and the manner of modifying crucial safety standards. Please include 20 cents to cover the cost of photocopying, handling and postage.

TIME TO REBUT ANTI-AIR BAG ADS!

A fairness doctrine complaint seeking time to rebut anti-air bag television advertisements of the Ford Motor Company was filed 7/14/71 with the Federal Communications Commission by the Stern Community Law Firm, on behalf of the Center for Auto Safety.

The complaint charges that ads aired by ABC and NBC present a one-sided, controversial and inaccurate picture of the air bag automobile safety device. Please include 20 cents to cover the cost of photocopying, handling and postage.

CENTER RELEASE SUPPORTS AIR BAGS!

The Center feels that more than 200 lives could have been saved Memorial Day, 1970, if quick-inflating air bags were installed in vehicles as standard safety equipment. This release supports air bags as standard safety equipment in all automobiles. Please include 20 cents to cover the cost of photocopying, handling and postage.

CENTER REBUTS AMERICAN AUTOMOBILE ASSOCIATION POSITION ON AIR BAG AUTO SAFETY DEVICE!

A release, dated July 23, 1971, answers an attack by the American Automobile Association on the Center's support of the air bag auto safety device. Please include 30 cents to cover the cost of photocopying, handling and postage.

RECOMMENDATIONS REGARDING WINDSHIELDS!

These recommendations of the Center for Auto Safety dated November 30, 1972 are addressed to the National Highway Traffic Safety Administration and include recommended changes in standards for windshield safety—zone of protection, forward control vehicles, rearward displacement of the hood in crashes (penetrating the windshield).

Also attached are letters received from the public to support the Center's recommendations regarding windshields. Please include $1.00 to cover the cost of photocopying, handling and postage.

CENTER RECOMMENDATIONS ON LAMPS, REFLECTIVE DEVICES AND ASSOCIATED EQUIPMENT!

The recommendations to the National Highway Traffic Safety Administration from the Center dated January 18, 1973 are based on consultations with experts on statistics as applied to variations in manufacturing processes affecting product performance or quality. Topics covered are Prejudgment of Issues, Objectivity, Statistical Validity (manufacturing, compliance, etc.). Please include 70 cents to cover the cost of photocopying, handling and postage.

COMPLAINT FILED AGAINST THE NATION'S TWO LARGEST TIRE MANUFACTURERS!

On July 8, 1973, the Center filed a complaint with the Federal Trade Commission against Goodyear and Firestone for false and misleading advertising. This release is a summary of that complaint regarding Goodyear's "polysteel" and Firestone's "steel-belted tires". Please include 10 cents.

CENTER APPLAUDS RAPID WORK OF THE NATIONAL HIGHWAY TRAFFIC SAFETY ADMINISTRATION PROPOSING NEW TEST DUMMY SPECIFICATIONS!

In a letter to the National Highway Traffic Safety Administration dated May 15, 1973, the

Center applauds the relatively rapid work of the Safety Administration in proposing new test dummy specifications and raises several questions. Please include 10 cents to cover the cost of photocopying, handling and postage.

CENTER RECOMMENDATIONS ON BUS PASSENGER SEATING AND CRASH PROTECTION!

These recommendations to the National Highway Traffic Safety Administration regarding bus passenger seating and crash protection include the need for greater crash-worthiness in school bus bodies, side and rear facing seats, seat belt assemblies in school buses, and more. Please include 30 cents to cover the cost of photocopying, handling and postage.

LYNDA McDONNELL OF THE CENTER FOR AUTO SAFETY APPEARS BEFORE THE SENATE SUBCOMMITTEE ON HOUSING AND URBAN AFFAIRS

Lynda McDonnell is a member of the staff of the Center for Auto Safety. She appeared before the Senate Subcommittee on Housing and Urban Affairs on July 24, 1973 to testify on the findings of an intensive study of the mobile home industry. This release is her testimony. Please include $1.10 to cover the cost of photocopying, handling and postage.

LETTER TO THE NATIONAL HIGHWAY TRAFFIC SAFETY ADMINISTRATION ON SUSPENSION SYSTEMS

On July 19, 1973, the Center expressed its shock and dismay at many of the NHTSA survey findings on the suspension systems of motor homes and pickup trucks with camper bodies. They also expressed their disturbance at the feebleness of the NHTSA's reaction to these findings. Please include 30 cents to cover the cost of photocopying, handling and postage.

RALPH NADER AND CENTER FOR AUTO SAFETY CRITICIZE SNOWMOBILE INDUSTRY AND URGE CONTROLS!

A Center release, dated May 14, 1972, sharply criticizes the snowmobile industry for its poor record of vehicle safety and environmental concern, and charge the industry with profiting at the expense of the public. The release is a summary of a 60-page report by the Center's Washington office staff, working in close association with Ralph Nader. Please include 20 cents to cover the cost of photocopying, handling and postage.

CENTER RELEASE ON ADEQUACY OF MOTORCYCLE HELMETS!

In a letter to the National Highway Traffic Safety Administration, dated August 22, 1972, the Center states that of the 75 helmets tested by the American National Standards Institute only 8 met the minimum Institute standards. The letter questions the delay in the release of these findings. Please include 20 cents to cover the cost of photocopying, handling and postage.

CENTER REPORT ON ODOMETER TURNBACK!

This valuable report on odometer turnback by a Center staff member covers the nature of the problem, extent of the problem, data studies, newspaper studies, state legislation, criticism of states allowing turnback, Federal Act (content, operation, deficiencies), findings and recommendations and summary. Please include $1.30 to cover the cost of photocopying, handling and postage.

CENTER REPORTS ON ADVERTISING CLAIMS WITHOUT SUBSTANTIATION!

In a letter to Miles W. Kirkpatrick, Chairman, Federal Trade Commission, the Center reports on the failure of the auto industry to substantiate their advertising claims, and the Federal Trade Commission failure to protect consumers from deception. Please include 60 cents to cover the cost of photocopying, handling and postage.

CENTER RELEASE REPORTS DELAY OF DEPARTMENT OF TRANSPORTATION TO INITIATE RECALL CAMPAIGN FOR TWO SAFETY DEFECTS

In a letter to Mr. Douglas W. Toms, dated June 8, 1972, the Center inquires into the delay of the recall of two cars with safety defects, namely, the windshield wiper arm attachment in 1947-1969 Volkswagens and the plastic locking grommet for the shoulder harness in 1970 and 1971 Ford products. Please include 20 cents to cover the cost of postage, handling and photocopying.

STEERING LOCK-UP DEFECTS ON 1971 AND 1972 FULL-SIZE GENERAL MOTORS PASSENGER CARS!

The purpose of this letter to Claude S. Brinegar, Secretary of Transportation, dated January 20, 1973, is to ask him to give immediate consideration to a safety defect affecting 3.5 million motor vehicles. The defect is on 1971 and 1972 full-size General Motors passenger cars. It urges the Department of Transportation to consider the lives of the many motorists and pedestrians being risked. Please include 20 cents to cover the cost of photocopying, handling and postage.

STATEMENT ON GENERAL MOTORS' RECALL OF 3.7 MILLION VEHICLES!

The third largest recall in history seriously downplays the gravity of the steering lock-up defect involving 3.7 million vehicles. The Center urges that letters sent by General Motors' divisions to owners alerting them of the hazard will indicate more fully the circumstances under which lock-up occurs. Please include 10 cents to cover the cost of photocopying, handling and postage.

CENTER FOR AUTO SAFETY DOCUMENTS GENERAL MOTORS' COVER-UP OF SERIOUS SAFETY DEFECT!

This release outlines a detailed, 21-page report documenting General Motors' decision not to conduct a recall campaign for a serious fire hazard in 1969 and 1970 Cadillacs. These two pages contain a brief summary of what is contained in that report and how a copy can be obtained. Please include 20 cents to cover the cost of photocopying, handling and postage.

RELEASE CHARGES GENERAL MOTORS COVERUP!

The Center questions the accuracy of General Motors' response to Cadillac defect reports. A letter to the Secretary of Transportation charges that GM Headquarters made two crucial changes in its policies on disposition of product failure records. Please include 10 cents to cover the cost of photocopying, handling and postage.

SUGGESTIONS FOR IMPOSING FULLEST PENALTIES UNDER CIVIL AND CRIMINAL LAW AGAINST GENERAL MOTORS OFFICIALS!

The Center for Auto Safety in this release tells how it urged the House Subcommittee to impose the fullest penalties under civil and criminal law against General Motors' officials. The reason was GM's continued non-recall of 1959 and 1960 Cadillacs prone to catastrophic steering failures. The release tells of ten internal GM lab reports to the House Subcommittee on Commerce and Finance and a 12-page report submitted by the Center to the Subcommittee. Please include 30 cents to cover the cost of photocopying, handling and postage.

CENTER ASKS COLE OF GENERAL MOTORS TO RECALL 1971 AND 1972 FULL-SIZED GM CARS FOR REPAIR OF A STEERING DEFECT!

In a release dated July 17, 1973, the Center gives valuable facts regarding a letter to E. Cole, President of General Motors, regarding a request to recall 1971 and 1972 full-sized GM cars for repair of a steering lock-up defect. Please include 10 cents to cover the cost of photocopying, handling and postage.

CENTER FOR AUTO SAFETY LABELS CADILLAC ELDORADOS "LUXURY LUG LOSERS"!

This 40-page report, dated July 26, 1973, details failures in 1967-1970 Cadillac Eldorados' front wheels which are prone to snap their lugs, sometimes causing a front wheel to fall off the car. The report, "Standard of the World—The Luxury Lug Loser," is based on secret General Motors documents. This release is a summary of that report. Please include 30 cents to cover the cost of photocopying, handling and postage.

GENERAL MOTORS VAUXHALL FIRENZA— A MOTORING NIGHTMARE!

This Center For Auto Safety release is a fascinating report of the tragedy many Vauxhall Firenza owners faced when the car was discontinued. It is another case study of how consumers both here and abroad have become the victims of the automotive industry. Details of how you can obtain a full copy (24 pages) of an Automobile Protection Association report detailing both safety-related and performance-related problems in General Motors' Vauxhall Firenza are contained in this release. Please include 40 cents to cover the cost of photocopying, handling and postage.

CENTER STATES BUICK-OPEL DEFECTS TO RICHARD C. GERSTENBERG, GENERAL MOTORS' CHAIRMAN!

In a letter dated April 28, 1972, the Center attempts to alert Richard C. Gerstenberg, Chairman of the Board of General Motors, to the abysmal record the Buick-Opel has accumulated. A number of Opel defects are given. Please include 50 cents.

CENTER RELEASE ON CHEVROLET VEGA—"THE LITTLE CAR THAT DOES EVERYTHING WELL!"

Evidently 500 or so Vega owners do not agree with that statement! Neither does the Center for Auto Safety. A letter to Richard C. Gerstenberg, Chairman of the Board of General Motors, dated September 1, 1972, gives valuable facts and figures on the production of the Vega. Please include $1.20 to cover the cost of photocopying, handling and postage.

CENTER FOR AUTO SAFETY REQUESTS EXTENDING THE WARRANTY ON THE VEGA ENGINE TO TWO YEARS!

This release of May 15, 1973 details the Center's request that General Motors Chairman Richard C. Gerstenberg extend the warranty on the Vega engine to two years, with no limitation on mileage. The Center urges General Motors to do so in recognition of widespread cracking, warping, and even exploding of these engines reported by Vega owners. Please include 20 cents to cover the cost of photocopying, handling and postage.

RELEASE CITES SERIOUS SAFETY PROBLEMS WITH VEGAS—ASKS RECALL FOR BRAKE DEFECT!

The Center lists several serious safety problems brought to its attention by irate owners of Chevrolet Vegas. This release is a summary of a letter to Richard C. Gerstenberg, Chairman of the Board of General Motors, regarding those safety problems. Please include 20 cents to cover the cost of photocopying, handling and postage.

CENTER FOR AUTO SAFETY'S AUTOMOTIVE ENGINEERING MALPRACTICE AWARD GOES TO GM'S COLE!

The first annual Automotive Engineering Malpractice Award went to Edward N. Cole, President of General Motors Corporation. The purpose of this award is to announce the name of an individual in the automotive industry whose actions or inactions have had the most detrimental effect on auto safety. A summary of defective GM parts is given in this release dated July 17, 1973. Please include 10 cents to cover the cost of photocopying, handling and postage.

CENTER FOR AUTO SAFETY GIVES 2ND ANNUAL AUTOMOTIVE ENGINEERING MALPRACTICE AWARD TO VOLKSWAGEN!

On July 24, 1973, the Center presented Volkswagen of America the Second Annual Automotive Engineering Malpractice Award. They singled out Volkswagen for the distinctive hazards of "The Thing", a jeep-like car recently introduced into the American market. This release outlines its major safety hazards. Please include 20 cents to cover the cost of photocopying, handling and postage.

CENTER FOR AUTO SAFETY CHALLENGES VOLKSWAGEN MANUFACTURERS TO A DEBATE!

Released on September 6, 1972, this report outlines the contents of the Center for Auto Safety's new book, *Small—On Safety: The Designed-In Dangers of the Volkswagen*. It is a study documenting how and why Volkswagens are unsafe. Specialists in engineering, law and physics combined their efforts which resulted in a clear, concise and illustrated report on the dangers of riding in a Beetle. Please include 20 cents to cover the cost of photocopying, handling and postage.

CENTER REPLIES TO *ROAD AND TRACK* VOLKSWAGEN ARTICLE!

The real question at hand is whether or not the VW Beetle is safe! A study by the Center resounds, "No!" Valuable facts and figures are reported in this release, dated March 9, 1972, on the safety record of the Beetle. Please include 20 cents to cover the cost of postage and handling.

CENTER TERMS VOLKSWAGEN WINDSHIELD WIPER RECALL A FARCE— AND ASKS EXPANSION OF THE RECALL TO COVER OTHER DEFECTS!

Find out how Volkswagen and General Motors are making a farce of the 1966 Motor Vehicle Safety Act. This report makes it quite clear why Congress should amend this Act. The Department of Transportation should have the authority to mandate recalls at no cost to the consumer. Please include 20 cents to cover the cost of photocopying, handling and postage.

DEFECT IN TYPE III VW'S LEADS TO UNANNOUNCED EXTENSION OF WARRANTY!

On August 2, 1971, the Center charged Volkswagen of America with failing to announce an engineering defect in the 1967-1969 Type III Volkswagens. This includes both the Squareback and Fastback models. A brief description of this defect and a letter to Mr. J. Stuart Perkins of Volkswagen of America give valuable facts. Please include 20 cents to cover the cost of photocopying, handling and postage.

RELEASE CHALLENGES VOLKSWAGEN ON VW BUS SAFETY STATEMENTS!

The Center charged Volkswagen of America with deliberately attempting to mislead the public in asserting that its compliance with federal barrier crash test standards provides passengers in VW buses with protection from front end crash crush. Please include 20 cents.

CENTER RELEASE ON FAILURE TO RECALL DEFECTIVE FORD PRODUCTS!

The Center for Auto Safety, in a release dated January 19, 1972, citing a new engineering study, hits the Department of Transportation on its failure to initiate recall of defective Ford products. Four million full-sized 1965-1969 cars made by Ford Motor Company had defective lower control arms. Please include 20 cents to cover photocopying, handling and postage.

CENTER URGES FORD MOTOR COMPANY TO RECALL 1965-1969 FULL-SIZED FORD PRODUCTS FOR LOWER CONTROL ARM FAILURES!

The Center, in a letter to Henry Ford, II, Chairman of the Board of Ford Motor Company, expresses amazement at Ford's persistent self-serving declaration that the lower control arms in full-sized Ford products are safe when failures are continually reported. Eleven such failures are cited in this letter. Please include 50 cents to cover the cost of photocopying, handling and postage.

NATIONAL HIGHWAY SAFETY BUREAU ALERTED TO POSSIBLE SAFETY DEFECT IN IGNITION SWITCHES IN ALL 1968 AND 1969 FORD LINES!

The Center for Auto Safety today informed the Defects Division of the National Highway Safety Bureau—the federal agency assigned with the task of investigating safety defects in motor vehicles—that it believes all 1968 and 1969 Ford lines have a design defect in the ignition switch assembly. This release gives valuable information regarding the possible defect. Please include 20 cents to cover the cost of photocopying, handling and postage.

CENTER FOR AUTO SAFETY RELEASE ON A SUIT AGAINST VOLVO!

This release outlines the plight of two justice-seeking owners of defective Volvos. One owner chose to file suit. The other had a suit filed against him for parking his vehicle in front of the dealership with a sign affixed to the car describing its repair history. Excellent reading! Please include 20 cents to cover the cost of photocopying, handling and postage.

CENTER RELEASE ATTACKS VOLVO FOR DECEPTIVE NATIONAL ADVERTISING CAMPAIGN!

The Center, in a letter to Stig Jansson, President of Volvo of America, dated September 3, 1971, charges that the expectations created by Volvo's advertising were not being fulfilled by either the car or the available dealer service. The letter cites dozens of documented reports from Volvo owners. Please include 60 cents to cover the cost of photocopying, handling and postage.

TOYOTA OWNERS DISSATISFIED!

In a letter to Iwao Kodaira, President of Toyota Motor Sales U.S.A., Inc., the Center covers the following: difficult starting and stalling, service, warranty work, alleged fraud and corporate responsibility, predelivery service, gasoline leaks and fumes, faulty accelerator linkage, brake problems, rear end whine, excessive oil consumption, unidentifiable noises and other annoyances. Please include $1.10 to cover the cost of photocopying, handling and postage.

Chapter 16

Consumer's Directory

WHO TO COMPLAIN TO IN THE
FEDERAL GOVERNMENT
  White House Office of Consumer Affairs
  New Executive Office Bldg.
  Washington, D.C. 20506

  Department of Transportation
  Office of Consumer Affairs
  400 - 7 St., SW
  Washington, D.C. 20591

  Federal Highway Administration
  400 - 7 St., SW
  Washington, D.C. 20591

  Federal Trade Commission
  Pennsylvania Ave. and 6 St., NW
  Washington, D.C. 20580

NATIONAL DIRECTORY OF CITY, COUNTY AND STATE CONSUMER PROTECTION AGENCIES

Attorney General of Alaska
Pouch K
State Capitol
Juneau, Alaska

Attorney General of Arizona
159 State Capitol Bldg.
Phoenix, Ariz. 85007

Attorney General of Arkansas
Justice Bldg.
Little Rock, Ark. 72201

Attorney General of California
500 Wells Fargo Bank Bldg.
Sacramento, Ca. 95814

Division of Consumer Affairs
Department of Weights and Measures
608 El Rio Drive
Oxnard, Ca. 93030

Bay Area Consumer Protection
Coordinating Committee
c/o Department of Justice
600 State Bldg.
San Francisco, Ca. 94102

Consumer Protection Committee
Room 303
City Hall
Los Angeles, Ca. 90013

Department of Weights and Measures
Consumer Affairs
Box 3575
Eureka, Ca. 95501

Los Angeles Consumer Protection Committee
107 So. Broadway
Los Angeles, Ca. 90012

Santa Clara County Department
Weights and Measures
Consumer Affairs
409 Matthew St.
Santa Clara, Ca. 95050

Consumer Protection Unit
600 State Bldg.
Los Angeles, Ca. 90012

Department of Consumer Affairs
1020 "N" St.
Sacramento, Ca. 95814

Attorney General of Colorado
104 State Capitol
Denver, Colo. 80203

Office of Consumer Affairs
503 Farmers Union Bldg.
1575 Sherman St.
Denver, Colo. 80203

Attorney General of Connecticut
30 Trinity St.
Hartford, Conn. 06115

Dept. of Consumer Protection
State Office Bldg.
Hartford, Conn. 06115

Attorney General of Delaware
Public Bldg.
Wilmington, Del. 19801

Consumer Protection Division
1206 King St.
Wilmington, Del. 19801

Department of Community Affairs and
Economic Development
Old State House
Dover, Del. 19901

Division of Consumer Affairs
794 Delaware Ave.
Wilmington, Del. 19801

Attorney General of Florida
State Capitol
Tallahassee, Fla. 32304

Commissioner of Agriculture
State Capitol
Tallahassee, Fla. 32304

Consumer Protection Division
1351 NW 12th St.
Miami, Fla. 33125

Consumer Fraud Division
Metropolitan Dade County
1351 NW 12th St.
Miami, Fla. 33125

Director of Consumer Affairs
264 First Ave. N.
St. Petersburg, Fla. 33701

Division of Consumer Affairs
Florida Dept. of Agriculture
Consumer Services
State Capitol
Tallahassee, Fla. 32304

Division of Consumer Affairs
Department of Public Safety
220 East Bay St.
Jacksonville, Fla. 32202

Georgia Consumer Services Program
Room 900
15 Peachtree St.
Atlanta, Ga. 30303

Community Relations Commission
121 Memorial Dr., SW
Atlanta, Ga. 30303

Director of Consumer Protection
Box 3767
Honolulu, Hawaii 96811

Attorney General of Idaho State Capitol
Boise, Idaho 83707

Attorney General of Illinois
160 N. La Salle St.
Chicago, Il. 60601

Consumer Fraud Section
Room 204
134 N. LaSalle St.
Chicago, Il. 60602

Department of Consumer Sales and
Weights and Measures
121 N. LaSalle St.
Chicago, Il. 60602

Chicago Consumer Protection Committee
Room 486
U.S. Courthouse and Federal Office Bldg.
219 South Dearborn St.
Chicago, Il. 60604

Attorney General of Indiana
219 State House
Indianapolis, Ind. 46204

Consumer Advisory Council
Indiana Department of Commerce
336 State House
Indianapolis, Ind. 46204

Department of Public Safety and
Consumer Protection
Room 2542
City-County Bldg.
Indianapolis, Ind. 46204

Attorney General of Iowa
State Capitol
Des Moines, Iowa 50319

Consumer Protection Division
20 E. 13 Court
Des Moines, Iowa 50319

Attorney General of Kansas
State House
Topeka, Kans. 66612

Consumer Protection Division
Courthouse
Wichita, Kans. 67203

Attorney General of Kentucky
State Capitol
Frankfort, Ky. 40601

Citizen's Commission for Consumer Protection
State Capitol
Frankfort, Ky. 40601

Division of Weights and Measures and
Consumer Affairs
Second Floor
Metropolitan Sewer District Bldg.
Louisville, Ky. 40202

Consumer Affairs and Promotion Office
Dept. of Agriculture
Box 44302 Capitol Stn.
Baton Rouge, La. 70804

New Orleans Consumer Protection Committee
333 St. Charles St.
New Orleans, La. 70130

Attorney General of Maine
State House
Augusta, Maine 04330

Office of Consumer Affairs
County Office Bldg.
Rockville, Md. 20850

Consumer Protection Division
Prince George County Court House
Upper Marlboro, Md. 20870

Attorney General of Maryland
1200 One Charles Center
Baltimore, Md. 21201

Attorney General of Massachusetts
State House
Boston, Mass. 02133

Boston Consumer's Council
218 Weld Ave.
West Roxbury, Mass. 02119

Boston Metropolitan Consumer Protection
Committee
c/o FTC
J. F. Kennedy Federal Bldg.
Government Center
Boston, Mass.

Executive Officer of Consumer Affairs
Room 905
State Office Bldg.
100 Cambridge St.
Boston, Mass. 02202

Massachusetts Consumers' Council
100 Cambridge St.
Boston, Mass. 02202

Attorney General of Michigan
Law Bldg.
Lansing, Mich. 48902

Detroit Consumer Protection Coordinating Committee
c/o Law Bldg.
Lansing, Mich.

Governor for Consumer Affairs
1033 S. Washington St.
Lansing, Mich. 48910

Interagency Consumer Commission
Office of the Mayor
City Hall
Detroit, Mich. 48226

Michigan Consumer Council
525 Hollister Bldg.
Lansing, Mich. 48933

Attorney General of Minnesota
102 State Capitol
St. Paul, Minn. 55101

Office of Consumer Services
Room 230
State Office Bldg.
St. Paul, Minn. 55101

Attorney General of Mississippi
State Capitol
Jackson, Miss. 30201

Consumer Protection Division
Dept. of Agriculture and Commerce
Jackson, Miss. 39205

Attorney General of Missouri
Supreme Court Bldg.
Jefferson City, Mo. 65101

Consumer Protection Division
155 W. Granite St.
Butte, Mont. 59701

Consumer Affairs Division
Dept. of Commerce
Room 315
201 So. Fall St.
Carson City, Nev. 89701

Attorney General of New Hampshire
State House Annex
Concord, N.H. 03301

Attorney General of New Jersey
State House Annex
Trenton, N.J. 08625

Camden County Office of Consumer Affairs
Room 606
1 Broadway
Camden, N.J. 08101

Office of Consumer Protection
1100 Raymond Blvd.
Newark, N.J. 07102

Attorney General of New Mexico
Box 2246
Sante Fe, N. Mex. 87501

Attorney General of New York
The Capitol
Albany, N.Y. 12225

Bureau of Weights and Measures
Consumer Protection
City Hall
Schenectady, N.Y. 12305

Consumer Affairs
City Hall
Long Beach, N.Y. 11561

Consumer Affairs
38 Brockway Place
White Plains, N.Y. 10601

Consumer Frauds and Protection Bureau
80 Centre Street
New York, N.Y. 10013

Consumer Protection Board
380 Madison Ave.
New York, N.Y. 10017

Consumer Affairs
County of Orange
Goshen, N.Y. 10924

Department of Consumer Affairs
80 Lafayette St.
New York, N.Y. 10013

Dept. of Weights and Measures
Consumer Affairs
399 Whiteview Rd.
Troy, N.Y. 12180

Office of Consumer Protection
County Office Bldg.
New Hempstead Rd.
New City, N.Y. 10956

Office of Consumer Affairs
160 Old Country Rd.
Mineola, N.Y. 11501

Office of Consumer Protection
138 S. Broadway
Yonkers, N.Y. 10701

Attorney General of North Carolina
Box 629
Raleigh, N.C. 27602

Attorney General of North Dakota
The Capitol
Bismarck, N. Dak. 58501

Attorney General of Ohio
State House Annex
Columbus, Ohio 43215

City Hall
Columbus, Ohio 43215

Department of Consumer Affairs
Lincoln Blvd.
Oklahoma City, Okla. 73105

Attorney General of Oregon
322 State Office Bldg.
Salem, Oreg. 97310

Consumer Protection Division
555 State Office Bldg.
Portland, Oreg. 97201

Consumer Services Division
Oregon Department of Commerce
Salem, Oreg. 97310

Metropolitan Consumer Protection Agency
Room 600
Multnomah County Court House
Portland, Oreg. 97204

Allegheny County Bureau of
Consumer Protection
209 Jones Law Bldg. Annex
Pittsburgh, Pa. 15219

Attorney General of Pennsylvania
238 Capitol Bldg.
Harrisburg, Pa. 17120

Bureau of Consumer Protection
Pennsylvania Dept. of Justice
2-4 N. Market Square
Harrisburg, Pa. 17101

Consumer Services
Room 210
City Hall
Philadelphia, Pa. 19106

Department of Transportation
8th Floor
News Bldg.
Scranton, Pa. 18503

Office of Consumer Affairs
Dept. of Agriculture
2301 N. Cameron St.
Harrisburg, Pa.

Philadelphia Consumer Protection Committee
53 Long Lane
Upper Darby, Pa. 19082

Attorney General of Rhode Island
Providence County Court House
Providence, R.I. 02903

Rhode Island Consumers' Council
365 Broadway
Providence, R.I. 02902

Attorney General of South Dakota
State Capitol
Pierre, S. Dak. 57501

Attorney General of Texas
Supreme Court Bldg.
Austin, Tex. 78111

Antitrust and Consumer Protection Division
Box 12548
Capitol Station
Austin, Tex. 78767

Attorney General of Utah
State Capitol
Salt Lake City, Utah 84114

Administrator of Consumer Credit
403 State Capitol
Salt Lake City, Utah 84114

Attorney General of Vermont
State Library Bldg.
Montpelier, Vt. 05602

Consumer Protection Bureau
94 Church St.
Burlington, Vt. 05401

Family Economics and Home Management
Room 210
Terrill Hall
University of Vermont
Burlington, Vt. 05401

Attorney General of Virginia
Supreme Court—Library Bldg.
Richmond, Va. 23219

Bureau of Consumer Protection
Inspections Division
City Hall
Virginia Beach, Va. 23456

Consumer Affairs
Dept. of Agriculture
8 St. Office Bldg.
Richmond, Va. 23219

Consumer Protection Commission
Arlington County Court House
Arlington, Va. 22201

Special Asst. to the Governor on Minority
Groups and Consumer Affairs
Office of the Governor
Richmond, Va. 23219

Attorney General of Washington
Temple of Justice
Olympia, Wash. 98501

Consumer Protection and Antitrust Division
1266 Dexter Horton Bldg.
Seattle, Wash. 98104

City of Seattle Consumer Protection Office
500 Municipal Bldg.
Seattle, Wash. 98104

Attorney General of West Virginia
The Capitol
Charleston, W. Va. 25305

Consumer Protection Division
West Virginia Dept. of Labor
1900 Washington St., East
Charleston, W. Va. 25305

Attorney General of Wisconsin
Dept. of Justice
Madison, Wis. 53702

Trade Division
Dept. of Agriculture
801 W. Badger Rd.
Madison, Wis. 53713

State Examiner and Administrator
Consumer Credit Code
State Supreme Court Bldg.
Cheyenne, Wyo. 82001

NATIONAL DIRECTORY OF PRIVATE CONSUMER GROUPS

Alabama Consumers Assn.
Box 1372
Birmingham, Ala. 35201

Kenai Peninsula Consumer Council
Box 2940
Kenai, Ark. 99611

Arizona Consumers Council
6840 Camino de Michael
Tucson, Ariz. 85718

Consumer Federation of California
2200 L St.
Sacramento, Ca. 95816

Los Angeles and Orange Counties Consumer Federation of California
621 South Virgil Ave.
Los Angeles, Ca. 90005

Consumers Assn. of Pomona Valley
Box 3
Claremont, Ca. 91711

Connecticut Consumer Assn., Inc.
1 Lafayette Circle
Bridgeport, Conn. 06603

Connecticut Consumer Assn., Inc.
425 College St.
New Haven, Conn. 06511

Dade County Consumers Council
1741 Southwest 4th St.
Ft. Lauderdale, Fla. 33312

Georgia Consumer Council
Box 311
Morris Brown College
Atlanta, Ga. 31314

Consumer Federation of Illinois
Room 1625
53 W. Jackson Blvd.
Chicago, Il. 60604

National Consumers Union
33 North Dearborn
Chicago, Il. 60602

Consumers Assn. of Indiana, Inc.
910 North Delaware St.
Indianapolis, Ind. 46202

Consumers Assn. of Indiana, Inc.
910 N. Delaware St.
Indianapolis, Ind. 46202

Iowa Consumers League
Des Moines, Iowa 50317

Consumer United Program
8410 W. Highway 54
Wichita, Kan. 67209

Kansas City Consumer Assn.
7720 W. 61 St.
Shawnee Mission, Kan. 66202

Consumers Assn. of Kentucky, Inc.
Box 1693
Lexington, Ky. 40506

Louisiana Consumers' League
Box 1332
Baton Rouge, La. 70821

Maryland Consumer Assn., Inc.
10202 Lariston Lane
Silver Spring, Md. 20903

Assn. of Massachusetts Consumers
Boston College
Chestnut Hill, Mass. 02167

Consumer Alliance of Michigan
Box 1051-A
Detroit, Mich. 48232

Minnesota Consumer League
Box 3063
St. Paul, Minn. 55101

Mississippi Consumer Assn.
1601 Terrace Rd.
Cleveland, Miss. 38732

Consumer Research Advisory Council
9000 E. Jefferson St.
Detroit, Mich. 48214

American Council on Consumer Interests
238 Stanley Hall
University of Missouri
Columbia, Mo. 65201

St. Louis Consumer Federation
6321 Darlow Drive
St. Louis, Mo. 63123

Montana Consumers Affairs Council
22 S. Montana Ave.
Helena, Mo. 59601

Consumer League of Nevada
1663 La Jolla Ave.
Las Vegas, Nev. 89109

Consumers League of New Jersey
20 Church St.
Montclair, N.J. 07042

Albuquerque Consumers Federation
Box 5219
Sandia Bead, N. Mex. 87115

North Carolina Consumers Council, Inc.
3608 Dade St.
Raleigh, N.C. 27609

Consumer League of Ohio
940 Engineers Bldg.
Cleveland, Ohio 44114

Ohio Consumers Assn.
Box 1559
Columbus, Ohio 43216

Consumer Conference of Greater Cincinnati
318 Terrace Ave.
Cincinnati, Ohio 45220

Consumer Protection Assn.
118 St. Clair Ave.
Cleveland, Ohio 44114

Oregon Consumers League
919 NE 19th Ave.
Portland, Oreg. 97232

Oregon Consumers League
3131 NW Luray Terrace
Portland, Oreg. 97210

Pennsylvania League for Consumer Protection
Box 948
Harrisburg, Pa. 17108

Consumers Education and Protective Assn.
6048 Ogontz Ave.
Philadelphia, Pa. 19141

Philadelphia Area Consumer Organization
1320 W. Hunting Park Ave.
Philadelphia, Pa. 19140

Alliance for Consumer Protection
821 Wood St.
Pittsburgh, Pa. 15221

Newsletter of ACCI
Dept. of Economics and
Business Administration
Geneva College
Beaver Falls, Pa. 15010

Rhode Island Consumers League
131 Washington St.
Providence, R.I. 02903

Monroe County Consumer Council
of the Genesee Valley
Box 3209 Federal Stn.
Rochester, N.Y. 14614

Consumers Union Inc.
256 Washington St.
Mount Vernon, N.Y. 10550

Consumer Assembly of Greater New York
465 Grand St.
New York, N.Y. 10002

Metropolitan New York Consumer Council
1710 Broadway
New York, N.Y. 10019

South Dakota Consumers League
Box 72
Brookings, S. Dak. 57006

Tennessee Consumer Alliance
Box 12352 Acklen Stn.
Nashville, Tenn. 37212

Texas Consumer Assn.
259 Walker
Center, Tex. 75935

League of Utah Consumers
425 Newhouse Bldg.
Salt Lake City, Utah 94111

Virginia Citizens Consumer Council, Inc.
Box 3103
Alexandria, Va. 22302

Washington Committee on Consumer Interests
Room 206
2700 First Ave.
Seattle, Wash. 98121

Consumer Assn. of West Virginia
3309 Noyes Ave. SE
Charleston, W. Va. 25304

Wisconsin Consumers League
7017 Dorchester Lane
Greendale, Wis. 53129

Consumer Assn. of the District of Columbia
328 D St., NE
Washington, D.C. 20002

D.C. Citywide Consumer Council
745 - 50 St., NE
Washington, D.C. 20019

Consumer Federation of America
Suite 1105
1012 - 14th St., NW
Washington, D.C. 20005

National Consumers League
Room 203
1029 Vermont Ave., NW
Washington, D.C. 20005

APPENDIX

Free Films For Drivers

Films are loaned free to schools, libraries, PTA groups, social clubs, organizations and so on. Or, you can write for them yourself as the representative or member of any such group.

After you have chosen the films that you wish to see, arrange with any group to which you belong to write and request the films of your choice. Or, you may write for them personally, giving the name and the group you represent.

When requesting films, please give exact title and type of film wanted.

Indicate the date on which you would like to show the film. You should also include a second choice of date.

Please be sure to return the films in the same container and at the same class of postage just as soon as you are finished with them.

Be sure to specify the size of the film you want (8mm, 16mm or 35mm) and whether you want sound or silent.

It is important to include the full printed name, address and ZIP code of yourself or the person within the group who is to receive the film.

Some film sources will send you a simple request card to fill in and return first.

While we have listed only one or two films that are available from any one source, you will find that when the sources reply to your requests, they will include a list of additional (and new) films that they will loan to you free of charge.

FREE FILM ON THE HISTORY OF THE AUTOMOTIVE INDUSTRY!

An exciting, entertaining and informative full-color film which traces the history of the automotive industry from 1900 to the present and into the future. A side trip takes us to the Indy 500 for the race and on-the-spot look behind the scenes in Gasoline Alley. Of primary importance is the sequence showing what car manufacturers and service shops are currently doing to increase car safety. Ask for "What A Way to Go!" when writing:

Bear Manufacturing Company
c/o Modern Talking Picture Service
2323 New Hyde Park Rd.
New Hyde Park, N.Y. 11040

SHOCK ABSORBERS— A MUST FOR ALL DRIVERS!

The first part of this full-color film reviews

exciting top speed events: National Drag Championship, National Outboard Races, Art Arfons' assault on the 600 mph land speed record, Riverside 500 stock car race and features the Indianapolis 500. The second part presents interesting and informative vital statistics about shock absorbers—a must for all drivers. Write to:
Monroe Auto Equipment Company
c/o Modern Talking Picture Service
2323 New Hyde Park Road
New Hyde Park, N.Y. 11040

FREE FILM TELLS ALL ABOUT DRIVING AND DRINKING!

An important film presenting the cold, hard facts about drinking and driving. It shows how drinking affects your driving ability and how you can motivate yourself to make the right choice. Ask for "Drivin' and Drinkin' " from:
Chevrolet Motor Division
c/o Modern Talking Picture Service
2323 New Hyde Park Road
New Hyde Park, N.Y. 11040

FREE FILM: THE DAVID HALL STORY!

America's Handicapped Man of the Year relives the car accident that crippled him for life. This award-winning film presents an unusually forceful message for drivers and passengers. Write to:

Employers Insurance of Wausau
c/o Modern Talking Picture Service
2323 New Hyde Park Rd.
New Hyde Park, N.Y. 11040

FREE FILM ON THE
SUPER 500 BREAKTHROUGH!

See all the thrills and spills of this tremendously exciting race won by Roger Ward. Scenes showing before-the-race preparation, as well as the miracles performed by the pit crew during the race, add to the interest of the film. Ask for "Super 500 Breakthrough" when you write to:
Monroe Auto Equipment Company
c/o Modern Talking Picture Service
2323 New Hyde Park Rd.
New Hyde Park, N.Y. 11040

FREE FILM PRESENTS
STORY OF A RACE CAR DRIVER!

The story of one race-car driver—what he does, how he does it and what makes him do it. We watch his team assemble and reassemble car and engine. We follow him through time trials and strategy sessions at the track and finally feel the excitement of the race itself. Write to:
Volkswagen of America, Inc.
c/o Modern Talking Picture Service
2323 New Hyde Park Rd.
New Hyde Park, N.Y. 11040